A CHURCH FOR SINNERS, SEEKERS, AND SUNDRY NON-SAINTS

A CHURCH FOR SINNERS, SEEKERS, AND SUNDRY NON-SAINTS

Arthur C. Tennies

ABINGDON PRESS   Nashville and New York

Library of Congress Cataloging in Publication Data
TENNIES, ARTHUR C. 1931-
A church for sinners, seekers, and sundry non-saints
1. Christian life—1960- 2. Church
I. Title.
BV4501.2.T423   248′.4   73-20029

ISBN 0-687-08050-9

MANUFACTURED BY THE PARTHENON PRESS AT
NASHVILLE, TENNESSEE, UNITED STATES OF AMERICA

Dedicated to the memory
of my Dad
Raymond A. Tennies
a country preacher
whose bequest to his sons was
"Freedom is to think for yourself"

Preface

A book is a bit of life frozen in print—a bit of one life that has been nourished by bits of other lives. And these other lives have also been so nourished—each life fed by others in an unbroken procession reaching back to the beginning.

When one aspires to be a writer and sees that aspiration partially realized in his first book in print, the honest response is gratitude and appreciation for all those who have contributed. As I have worked on this book, I have realized over and over again how the meeting of my life and someone else's has helped to shape my insight and understanding. While it is natural to be grateful and appreciative of those who were sympathetic, friendly, and supportive, I have realized that I should also appreciate those who I thought at the time wanted to do me ill. They may have meant it for evil, but God meant it for good.

This book was in my mind for a long time, growing and changing. Had I written it sooner, it would have been somewhat different from what it is. Had the writing of it been delayed, the same would be true. As my understanding and knowledge have increased, my views have shifted and developed. This book represents my best thought at this time. I intend to hold the views expressed only as long as I find reason and facts to support them. While some of my views are deeply and clearly held and have withstood the challenge of time, others are still cloudily formed. I sensed inconsistencies as I wrote. Whether the time will come in this life when all cloudy thoughts and inconsistencies are ended, I do not know, but I doubt it.

I was asked to write this book after some of my essays had appeared in *The National Observer*. I have been very grateful to its editorial staff—especially Roscoe Born, John Bridge, Paul Hood, James Meagher, and Edwin Roberts—for their willingness to publish some of my writing. Their kind words, encouragement, and suggestions have helped me greatly. I owe them a debt that I can never repay.

A manuscript, as every writer knows, is more than ideas put on paper. Mistakes must be corrected and slipshod writing caught and repaired. A writer needs help to see what he has written as others will see it. A neatly typed manuscript must be presented to the publisher. I have had the gracious help of my sister-in-law, Mary Tennies, who made numerous editorial suggestions and corrections and who typed the manuscript ever so neatly. My brother Herb, Mary's husband, has been more than willing for his wife to help me. I have also greatly benefitted from his ideas and suggestions.

If this is a theological book, it is what Dr. Edward Huenemann of the United Presbyterian Program Agency has called on-the-job theology. It begins with experiences and facts. Then it asks, "What mean these experiences and facts?" It is probing and tentative. It is incomplete and unbalanced. Yet it seeks to bring together the world of abstract theological thought and the world of human experience. It may fail as any experiment may, yet it can contribute to our understanding both of the world and of Christian faith. I have found stimulation and encouragement in the many conversations that I have had with Ed Huenemann and am grateful for the insights that he has shared and the kind words for my various writing efforts.

Every writer is shaped most by those with whom he shares life most intimately—and these also must help pay the price for the writing of a book, a price that the writer in his absorption may only dimly realize. I am grateful to Jan and for our life together. I have learned as much from what went wrong as from what has gone right—and she has too. We have discovered in our life together, although imperfectly, the meaning of Jesus' friendship. Our life together has brought forth new life—Diane, Linda, Susan, and Philip. Hopefully having me for an "old man" will prove on balance more beneficial than harmful. I am grateful to them because they have been enthusiastic about "Daddy" writing a book. I hope they are not disappointed.

I wish that I could mention all those who have contributed to my life, but I cannot. Even if I tried to list them all, some would be overlooked.

I do wish that my dad could have lived to see this book, to see his dream to be a writer realized in one of his sons. The dream to write was his before it was mine. I am an inheritor of both his wisdom and foolishness. I am grateful that as the years move on, my memory of his wisdom increases, and the foolishness fades away.

This book is a bit of life. Though I am grateful for all that I have received from others, I made the final decisions on what I would write—and so assume the blame for all that is wrong. If I have erred it is because I have tried to think for myself.

Contents

1.

The Church Is Not My Home

I wish there were a church for sinners, seekers, and sundry non-saints, but there isn't. At least, I haven't been able to find it if there is. The church, as I experience it in congregations, judicatories, ecumenical agencies, and national boards, doesn't seem to have room for such like.

I know some people will argue that the church is supposed to be for such. Jesus, according to Matthew said, "Those who are well have no need of a physician, but those who are sick. For I came not to call the righteous, but sinners" (9:12,13). And one could pile quote upon quote from the Bible. But they're quotes in the Bible. I'm talking about the church in the world—the place for the righteous, for those who have the answers, and for the saints. And I don't feel at home in the church anymore.

The church seems to be the place where one has to prove one is a Christian, where one can't be honest, where one can't raise any questions, and where one's motives are always suspect. I am beginning to wonder if being honest with one's self, being uncertain about what's right and wrong, and being weak are compatible with being a Christian—at least as most people seem to define that word.

The church presses in on me as a wasteland of non-thought and unexamined emotions. Toe the party line. Mimic the "in" phrase. Forget that the party line was the direct opposite yesterday. Hide behind the right words. Go along, the decisions have been made. Keep in step. Don't rock the boat.

I don't say this because I am writing the church off, dismissing it as useless. I believe that the church has been, and can be, useful. In spite of my not feeling at home, I realize that the church is of value. I know that it contains some hardworking, dedicated people. In the sweep of history, I can see that in spite of its humanness, its being an earthen vessel, the church has made the world a better place. If it has mirrored the worst, it has also mirrored the best. If it has been false, it has also been faithful.

But, in spite of recognizing its value, I feel like a stranger there, an intruder who doesn't belong, a ship flying false colors. Being part of the church is a burden to be borne, a job to be done, a sorrow to be endured. The joy has gone out of it. It's like trudging along on a weary journey on a cold, stormy, dark day. It is something to give to and not to receive from. It is not a place of help; for that I must look elsewhere. It is

14

not a place to meet God, but a place where one can try to do God's work. It's a going from God, like someone being sent on an errand. And the reward is to be relieved someday of the burden of the church.

Over and over I am made to feel as though I don't belong. Someone always wants to do something about the lack of quality in the church membership. We need better quality control in the church. The standards need to be raised. There are too many half-baked, half-hearted Christians. We need people who are completely dedicated to Christ. People ought to shape up or ship out. Too many church members are racists, male chauvinists, lovers of the status quo, immersed in the pursuit of the dollar, and—now that we have the Jesus movement—lacking in a personal experience of Jesus Christ.

It's not that I am in favor of church members being like that. If those people who want a better quality-control process get the job done, I'll not stand in their way. I'll just leave with the rest of the poor-quality Christians. It's not that I want to be one of the poor-quality Christians; it just seems as though that's where I'm stuck, in spite of everything I've tried to do about it.

I wish, then, there were a church for those of us who have seen Jesus far off, but haven't been able to close the gap; for those of us who end each day knowing that we've goofed again, and wake up some days not knowing whether being a Christian is worth it (except something about Jesus has gotten down inside us and won't get out); for those who know that they are racist and all the other things that Christians aren't supposed to be.

It's not that I think, as I will presently show, that the ecclesiastical quality-control experts are any better than we sinners, seekers, and sundry non-saints; it's just that they march to a different drummer. And they seem to have a monoply on Jesus. They always manage to wrap Jesus around whatever they say or do, so to disagree is to go against God. For me to march to their drummer would be to follow the party line blindly no matter the twists or turns or reversals, to abandon thought and reason, and to pretend that I am something that I am not. They have made the church for me a place where failure is not forgiven, doubts are not accepted, and unchristian conduct is not admitted.

So, the church is not my home. I'm just an intruder there. Not always have I felt that way, and not all at once did I come to feel that way. Step by step disappointment grew—and with it my feeling of being an intruder. What set me on the road of this pilgrimage to disappointment was not the individual in the pew or the congregations that I served. While congregations, as I have experienced them as pastor and participant, have contributed, they are not the cause. The cause has been my experience with the leadership of the church—the seeming inability of most of them to make constructive contributions in the midst of crises. Most of them are too caught up in the emotional confusion abroad in the land and have made the church a place where the issues cannot be examined and an institution that has little to contribute to the solutions of the predicaments we face. (And the church is no different than the rest of the world. Be it government, business, profession, or university—I see a wasteland of irrationality. This seems to be the age of damn foolishness.)

So I set out on my pilgrimage to disappointment. But long before the end was reached, I did what one must do with a blaring, bothersome radio—I turned the church off. I shut it all out and tried to think. Whether I thought right or wrong, I thought. For me, the right to think and decide for myself is central to being human. And I am sure that I have thought the poorer for having thought so often by myself. But for me to think and be wrong is better than to have been panic-stricken and right.

Now I have completed my pilgrimage. I just don't see any room for us sinners, seekers, and sundry non-saints. We cannot claim the church as our home; we are like Abraham. "By faith he sojourned in the land of promise, as in a foreign land, living in tents with Isaac and Jacob, heirs with him of the same promise. For he looked forward to the city which has foundations, whose builder and maker is God" (Hebrews 11:9-10). I accept the church as God's promise, a promise unfulfilled. But still I wish there were a church for us sinners, seekers, and sundry non-saints —a place for us stragglers.

I think there might be room for such as we, if only all the ecclesiastical quality-control experts would just accept one simple little fact.

17

2.

One
Simple
Little Fact

Perhaps I should not be so faultfinding and impatient of those who have not gotten hold of that one simple little fact. I was a pastor for ten years before I had it firmly in my grasp. It had played hide-and-seek with me all that time, sneaking around the edges of my mind like some amateur spy—never in the open but never completely hidden. Then one night it strutted into the center of my mind. It happened in this way:

An ecumenical mission project was started in the Midwest in the early sixties. Some of the program executives of the national missions boards decided that this project was what was needed to get pastors and congregations in step with Jesus Christ. Not wanting to waste time consulting with the local yokels, they hatched it in New York City and deposited it in a little midwestern village.

After five years, these executives grew tired of the project. It was tying up good mission money and wasn't producing, or at least not to their satisfaction. So, they decided to shut it down. The day of execution was set for the board meeting in October. (The board was divided between big guns—the national staff from New York, and local yokels—pastors and low-grade executives.) I was warned in the summer that the project was going to be killed. The United Presbyterian program executive told me that the national staff had gotten together and decided to kill the project because it was just a waste of money. From the way he talked, I got the impression that they would move in and shoot it down, like some outlaw gang riding into town shooting up the local saloon.

When the day came—a beautiful, sunny, warm, fall-colored one—I left early in the morning from Indianapolis. As the car sped toward that little village I thought about what was supposed to happen. I felt a sense of regret about the ending of the project, because I had come to appreciate what it could accomplish. To me it still had value. Yet, I looked forward to what would happen—I would see the big guns in action. I had spent so much time messing around in committees that couldn't make decisions—that backed and filled until one was nauseated. It would be invigorating to see in action some people who knew what they wanted to do, and did it.

I had a chance before the meeting began to chat with a couple of my friends. Being the possessor of inside information, I slyly and with a sophisticated air let them know that the project was doomed. When the chairman called the meeting to order I settled back in my chair to watch a good show. He explained that the purpose of the meeting was to decide on the future of the project, which I took as an euphemism for, "We're here to kill it." I waited for one of the staff members to lay it on the line. But nothing happened, not one of the big guns so much as cleared his throat. There was a massive silence.

Finally one of the local yokels spoke up. He had some suggestions about what the project could do in the future. Bang! One of the big guns shot it down. That was more like it. Somebody else had an idea and spoke up. Bang! Shot down again. After a few more rounds one of us suggested that the project be cut off. Bang! That couldn't be done either. Suddenly I was utterly confused. Hadn't they come here for that purpose?

About that time I noticed that one of the staff from New York was a professional shooter-downer, so I decided to run some ideas up the flagpole. Just as I expected, every one of them was shot full of holes before it reached half staff. For two hours we played this game. We pastors ran up ideas and the national staff people ripped them up.

After a couple of hours, it was time for a break. I maneuvered the United Presbyterian big gun into a corner out of hearing.

"Just what *is* going on?" I whispered. "I thought you told me that you guys had decided that this project is no good and you were going to close it down."

He smiled shyly and then said, "Nobody wants to rock the boat."

20

I almost gasped for breath. Rock the boat? I thought that was the name of the game. Hadn't I heard over and over again big-league church leaders condemn pastors because they didn't want to rock the boat, because playing it safe and not offending their congregations seemed to be more important than doing something about the injustices in the land? How could he stand there and give me that stupid answer?

We went back and played the same game for the rest of the afternoon. Even though I was completely confused, I tried to follow it in order to make sure that every possible alternative was suggested. By suppertime, we had run out of new and different ideas and were beginning to run up some of the shot-down ideas again. By the time supper was over, I had decided to rock the boat.

When the chairman began the evening session I said, "Mr. Chairman, I don't understand you guys from New York. We have brought up every possible idea and you have shot down every one of them. If I were one of you, I would come here and say, 'We have talked this over in our staff. I have been instructed to tell you that our national missions board will pull its money out unless you can convince me that the project still has value.' Or I would say, 'We have talked this over in our staff and I have been instructed to tell you that we will continue to support this project only if the following changes are made.' But you haven't done either. All you've done is throw out our ideas. Not one of you has had one positive suggestion or idea. I don't understand it."

The chairman stared at me. Finally he said, "Young man, you've gone from preachin' to meddlin'."

He then struggled for some way to get the meeting started again now that I had shot down their game. After a number of starts and stops, the board turned to a serious discussion of the future of the project, a discussion that lasted until almost midnight.

I had to go back to Indianapolis that night (and thus missed the crucial session of the board the next day). As I wound through the hills on my way home, my thoughts were in complete disarray. The words "nobody wants to rock the boat" kept running back and forth in my mind. How could those mission men from New York sit there and play that game?

As the turmoil of civil rights had swept across the land, I felt like I was caught in the middle. On the one hand, I had no doubt as to what the gospel required, but on the other hand I was the pastor of congregations in which a majority believed that all would be fine "if colored people would just stay in their place." How far could I go in being faithful to the gospel without offending the people of the congregations to the point that they would throw me out? I had a family to support. What compromises should I make? Always the booming voices of national church leaders condemned us pastors for not wanting to rock the boat. Every time I made a compromise, I could almost see one of them shaking his finger at me.

I was disillusioned. These men, who had made so much out of the church's being faithful to the gospel no matter what, had played the same game pastors played, the same game people played. How could they

22

refuse to face up to the decision that had to be made?

All this tumbled over and over in my mind. Like one of those frantic scenes in an old-time comedy where everyone is chasing everyone else, one fact chased another through my mind in the wildest confusion.

An hour passed. And then another. The car slashed through the night. Then suddenly the one simple little fact strutted to the center of my mind. I smiled. Why, of course, wasn't it obvious? These were people, and that was the way people were. Now I knew the problem with the church: it was made up of people.

I began to think about the congregations that I had served before going to graduate school. I thought about a session meeting and the way the elders acted. The board members from New York had acted just like a bunch of contentious elders. I had always thought that church members would stop acting the way they did, if they would just become fully committed. But now suddenly I realized that people acted that way because it was part of human nature, and that being committed to Christ did not eradicate this flaw in human nature.

The point is not just that people are not perfect, but that the vast majority of us who call ourselves Christians have massive inconsistencies in our lives. Jesus is quoted in Matthew as asking, "Why do you see the speck that is in your brother's eye, but do not notice the log that is in your own eye? Or how can you say to your brother, 'Let me take the speck out of your eye,' when there is the log in your own eye?" (7:3-4). Jesus' comment fits almost every Christian.

In fact, if one wanted the most fitting symbol of the Christian, it would be a person with a log sticking out of his eye pointing at the speck in someone else's. At one major point at least, almost everyone is non-Christian. I mean that what he thinks or does about some issue is an insult to Jesus. It is the kind of inconsistency that leads one to wonder whether that person is really serious about being a Christian, or whether he is just playing a game.

I could point to a thousand illustrations of this simple little fact. Martin Luther is considered, and rightly so, one of the great heroes of the faith. Over and over again he exemplified what a Christian ought to be. As long as there are people seeking Jesus' will in a hostile world, they will remember his standing alone against all the power of church and state and saying, "Here I stand, I cannot do otherwise." Yet Luther too had a dark area of the soul where Christ did not dwell, or perhaps I should say dwelt only fleetingly. In the midst of the Peasants' War when the poor were struggling for justice, Luther in a savage tract wrote, "If the peasant is in open rebellion, then he is outside the law of God, for rebellion is not simply murder, but it is like a great fire which attacks and lays waste a whole land. . . . let everyone who can, smite, slay, and stab, secretly or openly, remembering that nothing can be more poisonous, hurtful, or devilish than a rebel. It is just as when one must kill a mad dog, if you don't strike him, he will strike you, and the whole land with you." Even though Luther later regretted the savageness of the tract, he was so fearful of chaos that he condoned the suppression of the innocent—better to have injustice than chaos.

In the history of our own country we have the dark blot of black slavery. There were slaveholders who were earnest Christians, seeking to do Jesus' will in this world. They were compassionate and considerate of their slaves. But they saw no inconsistency, or at least never admitted to any inconsistency, between their commitment to Christ and their making people into property to be bought and sold. In fact they were offended by those rabble-rousing radicals up North who wanted the slaves freed, because these Christian slaveholders were convinced that a society built on slavery was what God intended.

But how many of these people up North, who were so sure that slavery was wrong, were able to see the wrongness of child labor in factories? Factory employment was often as brutalizing and inhumane as slavery in the South. At least one historian has said that there was a slavery system in the North as well as in the South, only in the North it was "dignified" by paying starvation wages. One can find among the factory owners of the North men who were deeply committed to Jesus Christ, who detested the slavery in the South, who saw no inconsistency between their commitment to Christ and the way their employees were treated, and saw no similarity between their system of slavery and that in the South.

Keith Bridston, in his book *Church Politics*, looks at the church as a political institution. In the prelude he compares secular and church politics and sums up the comparison in these words: "And the more I saw of it, the more I realized that compared to secular politics, church politics failed more grievously to meet professed standards of human conduct." Then he says that the difference between them is that church politics is less honest. He tells of his experience with the World Council of Churches in Geneva. "Many of the ecumenical politicians and their methods appalled me. It was difficult to understand how they could reconcile their obvious drive for power and their ruthless use of it with their Christian piety. Gradually I came to realize that, in many cases, it was not reconciled. They were blissfully unaware of any contradiction between their religious life and their political life." *

(And of course, this inconsistency is not something peculiar to church people. It is characteristic of humanity. One of my favorite stories is of the time when some employees of the National Labor Relations Board accused it of unfair labor practices. A few months previously the board had ruled that certain practices were unfair. When the board resorted to the same practices, the employees complained. What excuse did an official of the board give? If production was to be maintained, those practices were necessary, which I suspect was the same argument used by the employer in the case a few months earlier and rejected by the board.)

People are not perfect. Well, what else is new, one may sarcastically wonder. Isn't that obvious? Even my kids, when corrected, will often say, "Well, nobody's

---

* Keith Bridston, *Church Politics* (New York: World Publishing Co., 1969) , pp. 9-11.

perfect." But my point is this: obvious or not, it still remains that all too often this one simple little fact is not considered when we think of and talk about the church and its members. Otherwise, why would we be puzzled and shocked by good Christians owning slaves or running brutalizing factories, or Martin Luther applauding the slaughter of peasants seeking justice? For most of us, that simple little fact is not part of our thinking about the world and people.

Look at the ways people try to cover up imperfection. One way is to label people like those I mentioned above as hypocrites or fakers. The slaveholder "just played the game" of being Christian. Some may think that I was using *earnest, committed,* and *good* as words of satire, that I didn't really mean to imply that such were accurate descriptions of these people, but just the false labels they hung on themselves. I wasn't using these words in any flippant or double-meaning way. I don't mean to imply that every Bible-toting slaveholder was a committed Christian, only that some of them were—that some tried just as hard to be Christian as anyone who ever lived.

(I realize that many people will find it almost impossible to think of a slaveholder as a Christian. To us the owning of slaves is so incompatible with Christian love and concern that we cannot imagine not being able to see it. However, if one says that it is impossible, then he has said that being a committed Christian is impossible; for the slaveholding Christian is only one extreme example of what is true of almost all earnest believers—on the one hand there is a deep dedication to Christ and on the other a massive blindness to at least one part of the gospel. While I cannot claim that this is true of every Christian, I can say that it is true of all that I have known well. Also, I sense from time to time that I am more akin to the slaveholder than I want to admit. If I could see clearly, I am sure that I would be appalled at the gaps between the gospel and my own life.)

A second way by which people try to escape this one simple little fact is in creating the myth of the pristine early church. We are led to believe that, when the church first began, the members were completely dedicated; only later was the church corrupted by the world. Many people seem to find sadistic delight in condemning the church today for not being like the pure New Testament church. This idea that the early church was the golden age is a pile of nonsense.

Paul's letters to the church in Corinth show us a congregation made up of people who were far from the ideal. There was a lot of dissension, with many members squabbling among themselves, with Paul, or with whoever happened to be handy. They were often inconsiderate of one another, with the more affluent, for instance, flaunting their affluence before the poorer members. When Paul tried to collect money for the church at Jerusalem, many members were opposed to giving money to foreigners. On occasion some members got drunk at communion. Evidently many members were afraid of death, because Paul in both of his letters dealt with the problem. One member was having sexual relations with his stepmother, conduct that was even condemned by non-Christians.

A careful reading of James reveals a similar situation. It was a common practice in the church or churches to which the letter was addressed to give preference to the well-to-do, who were always given seats while the poor were told to sit on the floor. Some people thought that because they were saved it was all right to do as they pleased, no matter how inconsistent their actions were with the gospel. Many members were indifferent to the suffering of the poorer members, who often lacked clothing and food. Malicious gossip was common.

We know that there was constant squabbling between the Jewish and Gentile wings of the church. Many members of the church in Jerusalem believed that no person could be a Christian unless he observed all the Jewish laws, and resented Paul bringing Gentiles into the church. The conflict was patched over from time to time, but never solved.

The pure early church is a myth created by those who want to ignore the fact that people are imperfect. Church members, then as today, made a mockery of Jesus by their actions and attitudes.

A third way in which people cover up this simple little fact is the nice distinction that is drawn between sin and natural human weakness. When other people do things they shouldn't, it is sin—that is, their actions are inexcusable. They are doing things that Christians have no business doing. But when we ourselves do things we shouldn't, it is very different. Our actions are the result of very normal and natural human weakness.

Any discussion, then, of Christian commitment that would deal with reality must sweep aside the cover-ups and focus clearly on this one plain truth. Further, any description of how the church should function must suggest ways by which to cope with the blindness of Christians.

It is not surprising that we want to ignore the implications of this simple little fact, that we find it so difficult to think about the church and what it means to be a Christian dealing realistically with the imperfections of people. It is too theatening. What white Christian wants to admit that he is like the slaveholder at heart? What black Christian wants to admit that, if Africa had been the aggressive continent and Europe the passive, he could have been the slaveholder or the descendant of one? But also, it confronts us with a massive problem of reconciling the demands of the gospel and the reality of human nature without surrendering the demands of the gospel. Evil is evil, and it makes the world a hell no matter how many reasonable excuses and explanations one can give for it. A gospel that does not put the searchlight on evil and call people to a new life is no gospel at all. But neither is a gospel that that does not tell sinners of God's accepting love. How much easier and simpler it is to ignore the one obvious fact!

However, I am no longer willing to play the game of this cover-up. I have seen too much of the church and its leaders and members. I have no more illusions. I expect in my lifetime little better than what we have right now. If we are going to have a church, it must be made up of sinners, seekers, and sundry non-saints. I am willing to accept that, but I cannot accept the righteous posturing that is so popular in the church. When I see some church leader trying to make like Amos, all I can think of is a whore condemning people for having sex outside of marriage.

3.

People Can't Be Christians

Why are people like they are? Why the massive blindness in Christians? Why does commitment to Christ seem to have so little effect on most people? Many answers are given to these questions. The ecclesiastical quality-control experts assure us that it is because Christians aren't trying—they're just a bunch of goof-offs thumbing their noses at Jesus. But there is one problem with their accusation. I have had a chance to know some of these ecclesiastical quality-control experts and I have noticed that they have their blind spots too. Their accusation won't stand up unless they are goofing off too. The answer is really quite simple: Christians don't act like Christians because they can't. It's impossible for people to be Christian in an imperfect world.

Let me pause for a moment before giving supportive evidence for the statement that I just made. I realize that I have been using the word *Christian* without defining it. Worse than that, I have been switching from one definition to another. I have been using it as a synonym for church member and also for a person who identifies himself as a follower of Christ. I have also been using it as a synonym for a person who is perfect, one whose life completely conforms to the Christian ideal—whose attitudes, thoughts, and actions are in harmony with Christ.

Having admitted that, I wish that I could see the expressions on the faces of some of you readers. I can almost hear someone grumble, "Doesn't that dumbbell know anything about theology? Where did he get the idea that Christian is a synonym for perfect?"

I can almost hear someone else groaning, "Doesn't he know how to write? The worst sin in writing is to carelessly switch definitions." And I can see someone having a fit and falling through it.

I am well aware of the fact that writers aren't supposed to carelessly flip-flop from one definition to another. But I have noticed that these are the ways the word *Christian* is often used.

Also, I am well aware of the fact that *Christian* is not a synonym for *perfect*. I know that theologians have spent uncounted work-years trying to define what the word *Christian* should mean, and that almost all would begin by rejecting Christian equals perfect. But I am just using the word as it is often used. When I analyze how it is used, most of the time the definition comes out as Christian equals perfect. In spite of all the talk about defining Christian in terms of a relationship to Jesus Christ, it is almost always used to describe attitudes, thoughts, and actions that conform to the Christian ideal. The implication is that if a person is lacking any of these qualities, there is good reason to suspect that he is not really a Christian. So I am just using the word as it is too often used.

The reason people cannot be Christians in an imperfect world is that they are victims of that imperfection. Though it has been popular to see some people—especially the poor and minorities— as victims and the rest as exploiters, the fact is that everyone is a victim—rich or poor, black or white. Everyone is enslaved, and the problem for everyone is how to become free. A person is a victim of his childhood, of the system, of the need for community, of the pressure of responsibility, and of the splinteredness of society.

I realize that I will be running right by a significant question: Are people merely puppets dancing on strings pulled by forces over which they have no control, or are they able to make free choices? Probably a better way to put it would be: To what extent are the actions of people determined, and to what extent do they have the power of choice? I do not think that is a single question because people differ, so again the question should be rephrased: To what extent are the actions of this particular person determined, and to what extent does he have the power of choice? At this point I have no final answer, and I am suspicious of those who do. More than that, I do not want to get into that particular jungle. While I have learned enough to become convinced that a person does not have to be the mere victim of circumstances, I have also learned enough to know that the past and the situation in which a person finds himself are powerful influences. I am not necessarily claiming, then, that these victim-situations completely control a person, only that they exert tremendous influence.

Also, I realize that my emphasis is very lopsided. At this point I am concentrating on the imperfections of people, their failure to conform with the Christian ideal, and how these victim-situations cause that. I am ignoring good experiences in these victim-situations as constructive influences.

Every person is a victim of his childhood. The child remains hidden in the adult. The scars and burdens of years long gone influence the actions, thoughts, and attitudes of the adult. It becomes impossible, then, to completely understand any adult without knowing the story of his childhood. No childhood is perfect and many are inadequate. Maturity is, in large measure, the breaking loose from the bad experiences of childhood. The more bad experiences, the more difficult it is to break loose. Very few people succeed in gaining their freedom from the bad experiences of childhood. Many largely act and react on the basis of childhood-developed patterns. The rejected child very often becomes the angry adult seeking revenge on everyone around for his lack of love and affection. The scars of poverty are often carried to the grave even though the person as an adult may dwell in a mansion. The child hidden in the adult is the drummer beating out the rhythm to which the adult marches, and even Jesus with his tune has a hard job competing with the drummer boy from the past.

Kaiser Wilhelm II was, as far as I am concerned, one of the most tragic figures of this century, although I realize that many people see him as an evil figure. While I do not lay the whole blame on him, he contributed his share, perhaps more, to that disaster in August from which the world has not yet recovered. Wilhelm convinced himself, or at least tried to, that he was an emissary from God with a direct line to heaven. Otto von Bismarck sneered once, "How the Kaiser has found out what the will of God is no one can say." While one may be puzzled about how Wilhelm found out what the will of God was, there is no need for a person to be puzzled about why Wilhelm was enslaved by such conceit. Wilhelm was an unwanted child. His left arm, having been damaged at birth, dangled almost useless at his side. The damage had resulted, as far as Wilhelm was concerned, because his mother, out of puritanism, had not allowed a doctor to be called in time. His mother had later made it clear to him that she thought his brother would have been a more imposing ruler.

Wilhelm's mother was from England, and as a boy he visited his cousins there. They laughed at him because of his arm, his being Prussian, and his country's lack of a navy. The humiliating disdain that he felt from his mother and his cousins fueled a love-hate attitude toward Great Britain. At times he wanted England's respect and admiration, and at other times he wanted to beat her down, to get even.

Even though there was no need for Germany to have a large navy, Wilhelm forced his country into a bitter naval construction race with England and inspired his officers to look forward to the day when their fleet would fight and destroy the English fleet, thus creating a fear in England that led her leaders to decide that Germany had to be stopped. All this because he was still a little boy who had to have the biggest and best toys on the block. His childish antics kept Europe on edge until she blundered into war. While I think those foolish who blame the war wholly on Wilhelm, the fact still remains that had he been mature enough to choose chancellors as competent, wise, and fair as von Bismarck, the guns of August would have never sounded. In large measure the hell we call the twentieth century was the result of Wilhelm's being the victim of a childhood that he could not escape.

I remember an old man in one of my pastorates who had a simmering bitterness toward Roman Catholics. He soon realized that my attitude was quite different. Out of my respect for his age and his for my being the pastor, we had a tacit agreement not to argue about our differences, and usually avoided doing so. But one night at the manse after everyone else had left, we talked for a while over coffee. The conversation turned to our varying attitudes toward Roman Catholics. It was one of those too rare occasions when people don't feel defensive about their views, and are free to explain why they feel as they do. I sensed in him some ghost from the past, so I let him do more and more of the talking.

Finally he said, "I had an aunt who was Catholic. When I was a little boy she used to say to me, 'I wish for a day when I can wade hip deep through Protestant blood.'" He paused, and then added, "It's hard to forget things like that."

Tears came to his eyes. A man almost eighty, still feeling the pain of words uttered almost three quarters of a century before, still marching to the beat of an anti-Catholicism rooted in his childhood, realizing, if only for a moment, in the twilight of his life that it had not been right to feel that way. If the aunt had been there, she too might have appealed to her childhood as the cause for such words.

Second, every person is a victim of the system. If every black person can say that it is not his fault because he is black, every white person can say that it is not his fault because he is white. Each person is a part of a system, a culture, a piece of the world. It shapes what he is as a person. Cultural anthropologists have helped us to understand "that culture controls behavior in deep and persisting ways, many of which are outside of and therefore beyond conscious control of the individual." *

Even when a person is aware of the system of which he is a part, he is not free from it. The system seems to have a momentum of its own that enmeshes people. I have seen the agony of people caught up in the

---

*Edward T. Hall, *The Silent Language* (New York: Fawcett World Library, 1969), p. 35.

turmoil of the sixties. For instance, I know a clergy-man who was committed to living in a poor neighbor-hood. In a period of a few months he was robbed at gunpoint three times. He felt that these robbers were largely victims of their environment, but that did not solve his immediate problem. So he reluctantly decided to move to a more affluent neighborhood. He felt that he had no choice, if he was not to live in fear.

The system also has the advantage of familiarity. No matter how bad, a known system provides an established pattern for people to organize their activities. The familiar bad is always more attractive than the unfamiliar good. When people have to organize their activities, they naturally pick some familiar pattern. It is not surprising that the early church, as it established itself in the Roman Empire, organized itself the way it did, with its organization almost a mirror of the Roman civil government. This was the only pattern that they had to follow.

One of the interesting things about postrevolution-ary governments is that they are usually very much like the governments that they replaced. People are locked into a system, so when the chaos is ended, the old pattern is reestablished with all its faults. This is the reason self-government has been so successful in this country. The pattern was established over a period of almost one hundred years when England exercised only minimal control over the colonies. One of the important causes of the American Revolu-tion was the colonists' resentment of the British government's attempt to exercise more control. Once they had successfully resisted the efforts of the British government to bring them to heel, they reverted to the pattern of the past.

I read recently an article on Liberia. The author pointed out that the slaves freed from this country established a social system very similar to the plantation system in the South, with the Liberians almost reduced to servitude. These freed slaves organized a society on the only basis that they knew—the system in which they had been enslaved.

Third, every person is a victim of the need for community. A person fears to be different; he feels compelled to conform. Even if he does not agree with the group, he is afraid to speak out, to be the solitary voice in opposition. This is as true of youth as it is of any other age group in society. While youth may rebel against parents and the establishment, they rarely rebel against their peer groups. When a person does disagree, the group to which he belongs applies extreme pressure to get him back into line. Some recent studies have shown that this process of group conformity—what one person has called *groupthink*—operates in business and government, the escalation in Vietnam being a classic example.

People are made for community. Most do not and cannot exist as solitary individuals. Few people have the inner resources to endure the burden of being an outcast, even a person who has a strong faith in God finds it almost impossible. The writings of both Jeremiah and Ezekiel suggest that these prophets may have been mentally unbalanced, or at least were on the verge. If this were true, no one should be surprised by it. The burden of being an outcast greatly damages a person. Few people, then, have the strength to go against the groups in which they find community.

Fourth, every person is a victim of the pressure of responsibility. The teen-ager may condemn his dad for making compromises, but the teen-ager sees only one part of the predicament facing his dad. His dad has a family, including that teen-ager, to support. Being faithful to that responsibility is also important. The father cannot ignore that fact, when he must choose between sticking to a principle or making a compromise.

I once read in *The Wall Street Journal* an article on the Hershey Chocolate Company. Most, if not all, profits are used to support an orphanage, provide scholarships for orphans, and such things. The company has been frequently criticized for its conservatism. The reporter talked to one Wall Street analyst who was quite critical of the conservatism of the company's officers. Then the analyst paused and added, "You know, if I had a bunch of orphans to support, I would probably be conservative too."

During the sixties, many people condemned the denominational pension boards for their investment policies and their lack of social consciousness. The managers put their money into the safest and most profitable companies, seemingly little concerned about whether these companies made bombs for Vietnam or did business in South Africa, as long as they were profitable. When these managers were approached about putting money into economic development for

41

blacks, most of them refused. It is not surprising that the most conservative national church agencies have been the pension boards. The pressure of responsibility helped make them that way.

Fifth, every person is a victim of the splinteredness of society. Our society is organized on the basis of contending groups—one company against another company, labor against management, one party against the other, one lawyer against another. Without getting bogged down over whether it is the best possible system, it still can be said that at its best this contending group organization of society is a good system. We have an adversary legal system because our forefathers, out of their experience, concluded that such a system offered the best opportunity for justice. Every person, when he is tried, has the right to a lawyer whether he committed the crime with which he is charged or not. Even if the lawyer knows that his client is guilty, he is still expected to make a vigorous defense. In maintaining the vigor of the system and its long-term values, a lawyer may do evil in the short term.

Marketplace competition still seems to be usually the best way to decide what goods and services should be produced, and also seems to be the best way to get the best quality at the lowest cost. Economic systems organized in other ways find themselves with more problems and are being pulled toward the marketplace competition concept. But only a fool could be blind to the myriad of faults in our economic system. In fact, it might be more accurate to say that an economy built on marketplace competition is the least bad, rather than saying that it is the best. Most people have to earn their living in an economic system that often stinks.

When either management or labor becomes too strong, it is usually detrimental to the society as a whole. But neither is perfect. If a person is to be part of either side, he must support things that are bad—even though he may work for improvement on his side.

The political process too often degenerates into petty bickering and squabbling. Part of the politician's job is to attack and discredit the opposition. Sometimes he finds himself giving support to candidates who should never be elected. But in the long run, a vigorous two-party system with the parties evenly balanced is best for the country. Presidential landslides, for instance, are bad for the country. A person may feel that his party's presidential candidate is an ass. Yet to work actively for that candidate, to praise him for virtues that he doesn't have, and to try to convince people that he is not an ass in order to keep the other candidate from winning by a landslide may be the best thing that one can do.

In all five of these victim-situations, a person is under tremendous pressure to act and think in ways that contradict and deny the Christian ideal. And the pressure is too great. At some points, perhaps without even realizing it, his life scandalizes the gospel.

Even the most sensitive and committed person discovers that this is true. When he tries to choose the right, he discovers that life is a series of choices between alternatives and not a choice between ultimates. Only on very rare occasions is the choice between the Christian and the unchristian. Most of the time it is a choice between less than Christian alternatives. He is forced to admit that he can grab hold of the evil, but the good is out of reach.

One can say, for instance, that criminals are victims of the system; but what about the victims of the victims? What if the victim is a child reaching out for life, or an old person trying to eke out some dignity for his last few years? Which is worse, crime committers dehumanized by prison or people dehumanized by the crime committers? One can talk about and work for changes in the future, but what about the moment when the decision has to be made? Neither the person whose concern is focused on the crime committer nor the person whose concern is focused on the crime committer's victim can claim to be righteous.

The simple conclusion to it all is this: The person who thinks he can loyally follow Christ no matter what is a fool. He is just playing Peter. Peter, you remember, when Jesus warned the disciples that they would all run away after his arrest, proudly claimed, "Even though they all fall away, I will not." And you know what happened.

A person may sing:

> I'll go where you want me to go, dear Lord,
>   Over mountain, or plain, or sea,
> I'll say what you want me to say, dear Lord,
> I'll be what you want me to be.

—but it is, in large measure, wishful thinking.

44

If a person is a cynical pragmatist, as I am, he is tempted to dismiss the whole business of being Christian as a game of nonsense. Others may find satisfaction in riding around on righteous high horses pretending that they are conforming to the Christian ideal, but I do not. It is a game signifying nothing, or at the most, very little. Yes, I would dismiss the whole business except for one thing.

4.

If We Didn't Have Jesus, We'd Have to Invent Him

A pragmatist I aim to be. A cynic I have become. But I would look at the whole, at all the facts. And no matter how much I am tempted to despair, there is something within me that keeps saying, "the world has to make sense." Whenever I try to put things together in a way that makes sense, up pops Jesus. Whether being Christian is possible or not, I am still stuck with the fact that the world needs Jesus. To put it very bluntly, if we didn't have Jesus, we'd have to invent him.

I am not alone in this assessment. Malcolm Muggeridge, in an interview, made this observation.

"What does that mean for us today? That we have lost touch with an important reality, gone after false gods and set about to establish false values. We set foundations and study groups to work to find out what can be done to set things right. But none of it really works because, in my opinion, what must be re-established is a sense of moral order, of the kind that was previously derived from the Christian religion. We've lost that, you see. And so what do we do? We try all sorts of substitutes—drugs, erotica, great mystique of advertising and buying—and television is part of this, of course. But it doesn't work. None of it does. And this is how civilizations break up. It's as clear as can be. Seeing so much of it as a journalist, as I have, one has watched it all as a sort of voyeur, looked on with a sense of wonder at the predictability of it all. The parts are spoken almost to the word, the predictable thing said in support of this new folly or that. The voices come in on cue. Amazing."

Mr. Muggeridge sighs, and adds: "But ultimately quite depressing." *

Let me explain to you why I see Jesus as so important.

What one phrase would characterize this century for many people? The phrase I would choose is, "Life lived at the edge of despair." The thinking person finds himself at the edge of an abyss, dizzily swaying, feeling that at any moment he will tumble into the abyss, and then will be consumed by the despair. Even if a person has hope, he realizes that he must justify that hope by refuting the evidence for despair. The tug of despair is everywhere. It sometimes seems as though despair is the only theme of modern literature. Fact upon fact can be piled up to show the futility and meaninglessness of life.

---

*Bruce Cook, "Parading a Salty Sense of Morality," *The National Observer* (July 20, 1970), p. 21.

It is not surprising that this is so. What century has exceeded this one in parading the cruelty of people? Evil rides high and justice whimpers in a corner. People seem incapable of controlling themselves. We aspire to be like God—and sometimes it seems as though we are almost there. We have amassed power and knowledge. And now we can blow our world up. Technology seems to be like Big John. If the right one doesn't get us—a nuclear holocaust—then the left one will—a world made lifeless by the debris of our technology.

I look out at the world and see the insanity of violence. I cry to myself, "Where is God? Just what does he think he's doing? Why does he let suffering run wild?" Someone may respond, "Why blame God?" And my retort is, "Why not blame God? Isn't he supposed to be in control?" My retort is not one of thought and reason; it is one of feeling, of emotions churned by the tragic incongruity between what this world could be and what it is.

Is it surprising that so many have felt the pressure of despair—some collapsing under it and others trying to light some flickering candle in the dark? This is the century that started out with such hope and promise, and has since been one of hell and perversity. The major cause of it all is the July of 1914. Since those armies marched, disaster has followed disaster. One cannot help wondering what mankind would have made of this century, if that war could have been avoided. Ludwig Reiners, in *The Lamps Went Out in Europe*, traces the events that led to the moment when armies, like mad dogs, were freed

48

from their kennels. Then he asks the question: "Whose was the guilt?" His conclusion is that the fault was with all, and not just because these were evil men, but rather incompetent men. Then he goes on to show how each of the key leaders could have reversed the rush to war. He quotes Lloyd George: "Had there been a Bismark in Germany, a Palmerston or a Disraeli in Britain, a Roosevelt in America, or a Clemenceau in authority in Paris, the catastrophe might, and I believe would, have been averted."

I laid down the book and pondered all that. What if Europe had been rescued from the brink of war? Reiners believed "all in all, it is quite possible that peace in Europe might have been preserved for decades, had not the ship of Europe, fatally steered by weak and timid hands, run afoul of the Serbian reef." I think he is right. I can see the leaders of Europe, having had the door of hell flung open in their faces, tiptoeing in fear away from the game of confrontation. I can see the pressure of the people, as the facts drifted out, forcing the leaders to steer a new course. But it didn't happen. Why not? Why in all Europe was there only one competent man in a key leadership position—and he not at the top? Why couldn't one of those incompetents by mistake have blurted out the right words? And why couldn't God, just once, have interfered a little bit? Why couldn't God? But he didn't.

Sure, I can give reasons, but where does it leave room for God's love? It's fine to talk about people being responsible, but look at the hell they have made out of the world.

But the despair whose seed was World War I is more than just disappointment in the conduct of people. The foundations of hope have collapsed. One can build hope on one of two foundations, either a faith in mankind or a faith in God. Who can believe that there is an innate goodness in the hearts of people that, if once let loose, will propel us to a perfect world? But for many people, God is gone. There is no room in the universe for a heaven and a God. Even if they believe in God, what is that? Look at the world, and one can as easily conclude that God is malevolent as to conclude that he is merciful. In fact, I find it easier to believe that he is malevolent. Is not the world designed for cruelty? At least nature seems that way. Life seems to be a struggle in which the victory goes to the strong, and justice seems to be the cry of the weak who cannot win.

What reason then is there to believe that God— or whatever the moving force behind the universe —is other than what the preponderance of evidence seems to indicate? Why not believe that, if there is a self-conscious thinking force behind the universe, it is a sorcerer laughing at the tragic predicament of mankind—the more the suffering of people, the more the glee? And my answer is, because once upon a time something happened. There was a peasant named Jesus. From that day to this there are those who have looked at him and said, "There goes God." For them, to know what Jesus is like is to know what God is like. At one time then, God (or a part of God—and I don't want to get bogged down in the theological niceties) came right down on earth and lived a human life. A light was kindled in the darkness, and even to this day the darkness has not been able to stomp it out. Evil may ride high in the saddle, but it will never be able to conquer those who follow the light. The light says to us that God is love—he cares, he cries. The light assures us that the purpose for mankind is justice and peace.

I realize that many minds have wrestled with the predicament of life and have concluded, "all is vanity and a striving after wind," and that successful living is to escape to death with a minimum of tragedy. I realize also that many would say that my hope is just a dimly burning wick. Whether this Jesus is a blazing light or a flickering candle, I will not argue. I am well aware of the fact that believing in this light is no panacea. The evil is not swept away. The questions are not answered. The storm still howls. Someone may scornfully ask, "And what good has it done to believe in this Jesus?" I am not sure that I can answer that question, that I can refute the scorn. All I know is that something within me cries out for hope, saying life has to make sense. The only response I get is an echo from this Jesus—he is the only light outside to match the light inside. If I didn't have Jesus, I'd have to invent him, or die.

But is death an answer? It may be an escape, but I don't see it as an answer. In fact, death makes despair complete. It is the final defeat. If I have been able to understand myself and others, this is certainly true.

We have had in our culture, particularly among

the well-educated, a strong emphasis on this world. We, according to this viewpoint, should live life to the fullest here. And there is much truth to this. Emphasis on heaven later on has led people to close their eyes to injustices here. Also, if Jesus came to this world, we should be able to find meaning while we are here. But the problem of this emphasis on the world is that it ignores part of reality. Living a full earthly life is a resurrection of the Old Testament ideal—dying in ripe old age after having lived well here, with no life or a minimal existence afterward. The Book of Job was an attempt to deal with that problem. Life does not always work out so that we can die satisfied. Tragedies smash into lives. The corrosive powers of evil rust away life's meaning. In every generation a handful may reach old age satisfied, but for most it does not work out that way. Many people try and do not achieve. Children are struck down. Young men's lives are wasted in wars that were neither necessary nor wise.

If death could be confidently postponed to old age and if it only came when a person had lived his life to the fullest, then it would not be the final defeat. But given the world as it is, a person must come to grips with death. I am more and more convinced that to look for a life beyond this one— for some continuity of self-conscious personality—is not an escape from this world but a way of finding new meaning for it. The answer is not death, rather it is the belief that life will survive the grave, the hope and trust in life's final victory, the attempt to make enduring worthwhile. I, like Paul, would say that if death is the end, "Let us eat and drink, for tomorrow we die." If it is not the end, then the pursuit of justice is worthwhile, whether that pursuit accomplishes much or little, because the victory will come.

Yet how are we to know or to believe that life survives the grave? Again, our probing of the universe has robbed us of heaven. People of old may have looked at the night sky and believed that the stars were fastened on the bottom of heaven, but we know better. We have scanned the edge of the universe and have found no heaven. But we are looking in the wrong direction. The place to look is not in the sky but in the empty tomb. We believe because Jesus is risen from the dead. We depend on the witness of the first Christians. And that is part of the problem —we, who are sophisticated, are having to depend on the word of a bunch of peasants. But we have no choice. There is something within us, or at least something within me, that says, "Life must reach beyond the grave." If I didn't have Jesus, I'd have to invent him.

Meaningful living is threatened by other things too. How will guilt be assuaged? We have a conscience, or at least most people do. While we may praise the value of conscience, we also want to curse the burden of it. The conflict between what we ought to be and what we are, and between what we should have done and what we did, often becomes too great. We often escape the burden by the use of scapegoats, and condemning others. But what happens when that is not enough, or when we can no longer avoid facing the burden of our guilt? Most of us, at least once in our lives, do something so wrong that self-respect is shattered. Shame, like some poisonous cloud of gas, envelops us. We cannot die and we cannot live. We know that the wrongness will follow after us the rest of our lives. What will save us from lives darkened and spoiled by evil deeds?

Vietnam is such a wrongness. I believe that almost all of us past thirty are implicated in that wrongness. I see many who want to play Pilate and wash their hands professing their innocence. The air is heavy with righteous indignation as people scramble for a pure ledge from which they can pour blame on others. There is almost a desperate search for culprits, to find evil persons who can be blamed. While many can indulge in the luxury of scapegoating, there are some who cannot. Some are too much involved in the decision-making; their confident self-image of righteousness has been shattered. What of these?

Many years ago there was a murderer. His name was Paul. He was young, righteous, and angry. He was so sure that he was right that he wanted to destroy all those who disagreed. He was well-meaning, but ruthless. On his way to do more evil, he was suddenly confronted by the wrongness of his deeds. His confident self-image of righteousness was shattered and he met the object of his hatred. His name was Jesus. Paul discovered an amazing thing; this person he hated wanted to be his friend. Even though Paul sought to do Jesus evil, Jesus sought to be Paul's friend. In the very moment when shame engulfed him so that he could no longer like himself, Paul discovered that Jesus liked him.

54

Paul was not the first one to discover that Jesus had some queer ideas about friendship. Jesus had gone around Palestine trying to make friends with some of the worst kind of people. Only the friendless could appreciate Jesus' kind of friendship, a friendship that lifted the burden of guilt. Paul appreciated it, and he was not the last. A whole multitude of people would agree with me: if we didn't have Jesus, we'd have to invent him.

Forgiveness has another side to it. It has something to say to the person who has been wronged. How can the wrong be righted? It can't if one means by that, how can the wrong be undone?

> The Moving Finger writes; and, having writ,
> Moves on: nor all your Piety nor Wit
> Shall lure it back to cancel half a Line,
> Nor all your Tears wash out a Word of it.

Whether one likes it or not, this is the way life is. All the efforts to right the wrongs—government programs, laws to assure equal rights, efforts of the church, even a sense of guilt on the part of whites —cannot undo the injustices done to blacks. The disgrace of slavery, the wrecking of lives because of the failure of justice, and the opportunities lost because the system was against them are facts that cannot be undone because we attempt to bring in justice now. The dead are not brought back to life because the lynch mob is punished. The person who loses a loved one in a faraway war does not have the loss made up because the leaders of that war are condemned. This does not mean that society should not bring in justice after the injustice, nor that it is not important. This does not mean that the lynch mob should not be punished, nor does it mean that leaders should not be held responsible. I only want to point out one of the very hard facts of life.

How then can the wrong be righted? It can only be righted inside the person, when he is able to forgive those who have wronged him.

I know that there are many who would disagree, who would say forgiveness is for fools. They would insist that revenge is the way to right wrong. Get even, and the score is settled. I have traced the history of revenge, and it is the pathway to bankruptcy and disaster. Look with me again at this hell we call the twentieth century.

Far back in the mist of history it all began; but 1800, or a little after is a good place to begin. Napoleon sought to rule all Europe. Germany bitterly resented Napoleon's invasions. At that time Germany was not a united nation, and so had been unable to stop Napoleon. Germany then wanted to even the score. (Even then, one cannot say that the fault was all on one side. France, torn by revolution, resented the attempts of other countries to interfere in her internal affairs, and found in Napoleon a man who could stop them.) When Otto von Bismarck became chancellor of Prussia, he pursued the goals of getting even with France and uniting Germany. When this led to war and France's defeat, a new round of getting even began. The German generals wanted Alsace-

Lorraine because this was France's invasion route to Germany. Even though Napoleon III was partly responsible for getting France into the war and for the poor condition of the army, France naturally resented being humilated by Germany and losing Alsace-Lorraine. France wanted to get even, and this was a factor in precipitating World War I. France felt justified in imposing upon Germany the humiliating Treaty of Versailles. Germany resented the treaty and getting all the blame for starting the war; and there were grounds for her resentment. Germany wanted to get even—then came Hitler.

Every time it was a matter of righting the wrong using revenge as the gateway to justice—until there was no justice, until the depths of despair were reached.

Whether forgiveness is popular or not is beside the point. The truth is not created by a vote of popularity. The person who cannot forgive is doubly cursed—by the injustice and also by the bitterness.

A few years ago, a friend of mine had a problem. He discovered that his wife had had an affair, and he did not know whether a daughter was his or his wife's lover's. As the tragedy tore at him, the question churned in his mind. Finally he saw that it didn't make any difference as to who was her father as far as whose sperm got there first. If she was to know a father's love, she would know his or none. He, would make a home for her and provide for her, not the lover. She would call him daddy and no other. When he came home at night she would run to him no matter how far away she was, as fast as she could with laughter in her face and rush full speed into his arms, almost knocking him over. "Daddy! Daddy! Daddy!" she would cry. And she would rush that way to no other. He was her father in the most practical way possible—they were thrown together as father and daughter. His love—not that of some surreptitious lover—even if he wanted to— would shield her, build her up, set her free for life. As she walked into adulthood, she would turn to say, "Thank you," or to curse him, depending on what he did. If he took her for his daughter, both would be the richer for it. If he rejected her, both would be made bankrupt. As God's steward, he was called to be father to her—no matter what the past, the sin, the sperm. It was his duty. It would be his joy.

I am well aware of the fact that forgiveness is not popular. I see the evidence everywhere, even in the church. Even there the gospel according to Washington (reward your friends and punish your enemies) is much more popular than the gospel according to Jesus (love your enemies and pray for those who persecute you). The evidence is overwhelming. Forgiveness is not practical. Expecting forgiveness is to expect the impossible. All this may be true, but I see a cross and hear a voice, "Father, forgive them, for they know not what they do." Practical or not, possible or not, in these words is hope for the world. We shall not know peace until there is a multitude to say, "Amen, how true. If we didn't have Jesus, we'd have to invent him." And a multitude who can forgive.

Our pride in technology has led us to believe that the major problem is how to harness technology for the welfare of mankind. But the major problem is not a lack of technology or of knowledge of how to apply it; the major problem is a lack of trust. Our technology threatens to outrun our honesty.

Let me put the problem another way. We are told over and over again all the marvelous things that can be done with the use of computers. To hear the computer scientist talk, the only barriers to this promised land of computerism are developing the technology and reducing the unit cost. But, the true barrier is lack of trust. It is not a matter of whether the scientist can solve the technical problems, rather whether we are honest enough to trust our lives to the computer.

For instance, there is computer banking. If a person wishes to make a purchase, he gives his card to a clerk who puts it into the terminal. The clerk then punches a few keys and automatically the money is moved from the customer's account to the merchant's. But where are the records? What is to keep someone from illegally taking money out of one account and sticking it in another? How can a person prove that his bank account has been tapped?

The Equity Funding scandal has made business painfully aware of what thieves can do because of computers. Computers are widely used in business, and business has probably never been so vulnerable to theft.

The computer only makes clear the problem of an interdependent society:

But the very fact that he has to depend on his fellow man has made the problem of survival extraordinarily difficult. Man is not an ant, conveniently equipped with an inborn pattern of social instincts. On the contrary, he is pre-eminently endowed with a fiercely self-centered nature. If his relatively weak physique forces him to seek cooperation, his untamed unconscious drives constantly threaten to disrupt his social working partnerships.*

And the more interdependent society becomes, the more dependent it is on trust. American society is not built on technology; it is built on trust. By trust I mean believing what other people say and having confidence that they will act honestly.

Consider for a moment just how much you can prove to be true. By prove I mean that you have made a personal investigation, and on the basis of that you are convinced that a certain thing is valid. Very little. Most of the time when a person says, "I know . . ." he really means, "I believe that is the way it is." We are utterly dependent on what others tell us. We are so dependent that we can easily be deceived.

Recently I read an account of the championship season of Plainfield Teachers College in the *Wall Street Journal* (December 5, 1972). A man by the name of Morris Newburger perpetrated a hoax on some of the leading papers in the country, including

---

*Robert L. Heilbroner, *The Worldly Philosophers* (Time Reading Program Special Edition, 1962), p. 7.

the *New York Times*. For several weeks he had these papers reporting the scores of games between nonexistent Plainfield and various nonexistent opponents. He was even successful in getting sports columnists to comment on the marvelous achievements of the team. He started the whole thing by just calling the sports desks of several papers to report a score. To his amazement they took his word for the score. But what else could they have done? If a newspaper only printed the news its reporter had proven for themselves to be true, even the *New York Times* would have little to print.

Newburger's deceit was harmless, resulting in a few red faces at the sports desks. But most deceptions are not harmless. They threaten the very foundation of society, the trust a society must have to function. Our society is threatened now. Too many lies have been told. I hesitate to mention the lies that attract our attention today—the lies of Watergate—because, by the time this book is printed, a whole new bundle may have been dropped on us. As each new set of lies is stripped naked, people's trust is eroded that much more.

Over against our all-too-easy attitude toward deceit which most of us frequently practice while condemning others for so doing, is the disturbing presence of Jesus. Jesus had lunch one day with a man named Zacchaeus. Zacchaeus was a dishonest politician. In the presence of Jesus, Zacchaeus felt compelled to break away from the deceits of the past. He told Jesus, "Behold, Lord, the half of my goods I give to the poor; and if I have defrauded any one of

61

anything, I restore it fourfold." Jesus' response was, "Today salvation has come to this house, since he also is a son of Abraham" (Matthew 9:8-9).

Zacchaeus had just been following the standard operating procedure of the day. He could very well have excused his conduct by saying that everyone did it. The same thing could have been said by Matthew. Every tax collector, or almost every, tried to shake down the people for all that he could get, profiting on the difference between what he had to send to Rome and what he took in. But the presence of Jesus called Zacchaeus and Matthew to a different way of life.

Many people today would argue that many of the deceits we practice are just standard operating procedure. If everyone, or almost everyone, is doing it, why should one person do differently? Yet the improvement in conduct takes place because there are people who are willing to be different. If conduct is finally determined by the lowest level of conduct, society always goes to hell. And the pressure to operate unethically is always present. Barnum's comment that a sucker is born every minute is too true. There are unlimited opportunities to deceive people, to trade on the trust essential for a society to function. Over against that Jesus sets a different standard. When a person looks out at our world and sees deceit piled upon deceit, when it seems as though the theme song of our age is to deceive before being deceived, the concerned person will say, "If we didn't have Jesus, we'd have to invent him."

Love makes the world go round. A few years ago

one would have had to argue that premise. Loren
Eiseley found it necessary to refute the notion "that
there are two kinds of people, the tough- and the
tender-minded," and that the tough-minded would
survive. He went on to argue:

The truth is that if man at heart were not a tender
creature in a peculiarly special way, he would long since
have left his bones to the wild dogs that roved the African
grasslands where he first essayed the great adventure of
becoming human.*

Halford Luccock, in his book *Unfinished Business,*
poked a finger of gentle humor at Bertrand Russell
for discovering in the aftermath of World War II
that the world's greatest need was Christian love.
Today one need hardly argue for the importance of
love. In fact it has become very popular to speak of
love.

Yet for all that, the world seems to move ahead
unheeding the need for love. Toughness, ruthless
competition, and the ability to endure all too often
seem the qualities needed for survival. In a hard and
ruthless world there seems to be little room for kindness and compassion. Love seems like a nun who
finds herself by mistake in a house of ill repute.

And the Church mirrors the world. I remember a
conversation I heard one day about a church executive who had failed as the head of an ecumenical

---

*Eiseley, "An Evolutionist Looks at Modern Man," *Saturday
Evening Post* (April 26, 1958), p. 120.

agency. One person gave this explanation of the executive's failure: "None of the pastors there liked him, so they crucified him." I thought to myself, "Well, we have learned something from the life of Jesus. If you don't like someone, just crucify him." The church has little time for weakness. Success is survival in the ecclesiastical jungle. I doubt whether any other institution has developed backstabbing to as fine an art as the church has. There is even a good passage of scripture for it. "And whatever you do, in word or deed, do everything in the name of the Lord Jesus, giving thanks to God the Father through him" (Colossians 3:17). The backstabbing is always done in the name of Jesus.

This is not to say that love is unimportant in the church; it is of the utmost importance. Love is to be trotted out at appropriate times. The successful minister usually seems to be one who can speak eloquently of love, but who doesn't get carried away by all that mushiness, knowing that nothing beats a good backstabbing job.

Love may be a grand thing to talk about, and it may be one of the deep longings of the human heart, but is it practical? Once upon a time there was a man who made it practical, and he built his life around it. Hatred beat on him and it killed him, but he never stopped loving. His love gave strength to people who were broken. He refused to become embittered by the hostility. On the cross, his last words were, "Father, into thy hands I commit my spirit!" Hatred killed him, but could not destroy him. Love was the victor, not hatred.

We look at the world and see the weakness of love; we look at the cross and see the power of love. If we didn't have Jesus, we'd have to invent him.

Embodied in that peasant from the past are the hopes and ideals of mankind. In the tragic chaos of this century his words and life are as new as the latest fad. Yet all too often he is a figure perched on the distant horizon. All too often he is a dream in the night. Can that dream be brought to the morning?

5.

Fleeing the Predicament

This is the predicament: On the one hand people can't be Christian, but on the other hand Jesus can only make a difference if he inspires people to do his will. Jesus, perched on the horizon while the world is hell, is no Jesus, no savior. He is just a dream in the night. That dream can only come to the morning through us. How do we deal with this predicament that what can't be must be? Any effort to deal with it must firmly grasp two realities—the need to be faithful and the failure to be faithful. We cannot ignore either. If we ignore the need to be faithful, we make the gospel meaningless in the affairs of people. If we ignore the failure to be faithful, we drive people to despair or hypocrisy.

Before trying to deal with the predicament, I want

to use this chapter to look at how the church has often tried to flee it. In fact, it is my judgment that the vast majority of church members have sought an escape from the pain of this ambiguity.

My cynicism is always tempered by looking at the history of the church. The fact is that Jesus has neither just stayed perched on the horizon nor has he fully entered the world through his followers. In spite of the failures of the church, Jesus has made a difference. The world is the better because Jesus has been at work in it through his church. Kenneth Scott Latourette, at the end of his massive study of the expansion of Christianity, states:

From that brief life and its apparent frustration has flowed a more powerful force for the triumphal waging of man's long battle than any other ever known by the human race. Through it millions have had their inner conflicts resolved in progressive victory over their baser impulses. By it millions have been sustained in the greater tragedies of life and have come through radiant. Through it hundreds of millions have been lifted from illiteracy and ignorance and have been placed upon the road of growing intellectual freedom and of control over their physical environment. It has done more to allay the physical ills of disease and famine than any other impulse known to man. It has emancipated millions from chattel slavery and millions of others from thraldom to vice. It has protected millions from exploitation by their fellows. It has been the most fruitful source of movements to lessen the horrors of war and to put the relations of men and nations on the basis of justice and peace.

But Latourette did not try to blind himself to the failures either, for in the next paragraph he added:

Seldom if ever has the triumph been clear cut and complete. The greatest saints are aware that they have not fully attained. The Church is divided by jealousies and strife. In its great forward surges the faith has been closely associated with movements in economics, statecraft, and international, interracial, and inter-class contention which are contrary to its aspirations. Again and again, even within the Church itself, the elements appear dominant which bound Jesus to his cross and he seems crucified afresh. Some of the hereditary evils of the race attain their most colossal dimensions among the peoples and cultures in which the faith which stemmed from Jesus has been longest represented.*

I don't want to get bogged down in a whole lot of tangental discussion at this point. Someone may argue that the church should have done an awful lot more. Another may argue that the church's accomplishments are so small compared to its failures that its history only demonstrates its uselessness. At this point I am only saying that the church has made a difference. (If a person moves a quarter of an inch, he has still moved.) Whether that difference is great or small, it still encourages me. The church has not been useless.

A look at the history of the church shows that the predicament really has two parts. One part has to do

---

*Latourette, *Advance Through Storm* (New York: Harper & Brothers, 1945) , pp. 503-4.

with how to deal at any given moment with the fact that there is a gap in every person's life between what Jesus wants him to be and what he is. How does a person live honestly with that failure? The second part has to do with how the gospel can enter a person's life in such a way that he grows and changes, his life becoming more like Jesus'. How does a person become more Christian? Or to put it another way, how can he both accept himself for what he is and still be encouraged to change and become a better person?

But even the way I have stated it does not fully deal with the problem of the gap as present experience. I am not talking about the fact that there is a wee bit of inconsistency between what a person should be and what he actually is. I am talking about the fact that a person participates in, encourages, and contributes to the evil that makes this world a hell. At significant points a person does not and will not do Jesus' will. He may be oblivious that he is not doing Jesus' will. Even if he is aware of it, he feels compelled to say to Jesus, "No!"

One can always say, "Well, Jesus understands; nobody's perfect." And what is that supposed to mean— that it's OK with Jesus? Let's get practical about the matter. Suppose a black family moves into a suburb and their white neighbor is so prejudiced that he won't let his kids play with the new kids. Suppose that the neighbor's prejudice encourages his kids and the other white kids on the block to make life miserable for the black kids. And suppose the neighbor says, "I'm sorry, but I'm so scared of blacks that I just can't have my kids playing with them." What's Jesus supposed to do—go over and wipe away the tears and help those black kids understand why their neighbor is such an SOB?

I realize that some will immediately respond, "Why, the action of the neighbor is inexcusable! That man's no Christian." But—and I hope I don't have to repeat the whole argument of chapters 2 and 3—that man *is everyone*. True, many Christians would act Christian in the above situation, but how about the points where they are the SOBs—either being oblivious to their SOBism, or saying no to Jesus?

It is this fact, the fact of SOBism, that has driven church members through the centuries to find an escape from the predicament. A person is asked to face honestly the full truth about himself; most people can't stand that much honesty. Only on rare occasions have there been people in the church who were able to be honest with themselves and advocate it for others. The apostle Paul was, and he was bitterly attacked by others in the church. From time to time a voice has been heard saying, "Paul was right." But the voice has been quickly drowned out by other voices. So the church has spent most of its history looking for mechanisms by which to escape.

The predicament forces a person to face the question of whether he is really loyal to Jesus. Most church members seek some way to prove their loyalty; persecution has been one way. The persecuted church member has always attracted the admiration of many others. I mention in chapter 2 the blind spot in Martin Luther's life. Why is it that we can so easily overlook his major failure? We can, because he proved his loyalty to Jesus. As long as there are people who want to be Christians, there will be those who will praise Luther for his ringing words, "Here I stand!" It is not surprising that Dietrich Bonhoeffer has been so much admired. Here again was a church member who was willing to be loyal no matter what—even unto death. Many people look back to the early church as the golden age of Christianity. They overlook all the failings of these early church members and only remember that there was a time when many had to endure persecution from neighbors and state because of their loyalty to Jesus.

The person who is willing to die for his faith, no matter what his failings, must be counted as one of the loyal disciples of Jesus. It is true that the quality of church membership would probably improve if the church was not so popular. If people had to pay some price in terms of economic disadvantage, condemnation by neighbors, or threat by government, becoming openly identified as a follower of Jesus would be taken more seriously. The average person would probably only take that step after very careful thought. Once having taken it, he would be less likely to back away from his commitment. It is not surprising, then, that a cult of nostalgia for the persecuted church has developed in America.

While it is true that persecution often improves the quality of church members, it is not so easy to decide whether a suffering church is more effective than a prosperous one. Which would be better, a Germany with the evils of Hitler and a Bonhoeffer, or a Germany without Hitler and with a bunch of lackadaisical church members? I don't want to debate the point here. I only want to indicate that a time of persecution does not solve the problem of evil in the world, and nostalgia for the persecuted church is just one mechanism for escaping the predicament.

In a sense, whether the church is better off persecuted or prosperous is irrelevant. It has often not been persecuted, and being a member has been the thing to do. What then? How does one prove his loyalty to Jesus and thus have a way of dealing with the predicament? Throughout the history of the church one answer has been to become a minister, priest, or missionary. Again it is not surprising that many of the most earnest and deeply committed church members have chosen this route, wanting to spend full time in the work of the church—and to the benefit of the church. I think that much of the credit for whatever improvement Christianity has made in the world must go to that host of dedicated men and women who through the years have tried to persuade their fellows to take Jesus more seriously and to pattern their lives after him. Yet, when a person feels that, because he is a minister, priest, or missionary, he has solved the predicament, he is using the ministry as an escape mechanism. The minister, if he is honest, must say, "I, too, have denied Jesus."

The most popular way of dealing with the predicament has been making rules. Each generation has had its ecclesiastical quality-control experts who have found great personal satisfaction in condemning the majority of church members and loudly calling for a set of rules, so that members will either shape up or be shipped out. The problem has always been: What rules will be enforced and which ignored? It always comes down to that because it is impossible for anyone to be perfect.

While I can become quite resentful of what I call the ecclesiastical quality-control experts, I must admit that they represent an inevitable tendency in the church, often focusing on a major evil.

For instance, consider the traditionally strong opposition in some denominations, such as the Methodists, to the use of liquor. On the frontier in the eighteenth century the excessive use of liquor was a major problem. When the circuit riders were confronted over and over with the many lives that were ruined, families that were wrecked, and communities that were destroyed because of excessive drunkenness, it is not surprising that the use of liquor was seen as a major evil. The Methodists only did what the church usually does—attack a pressing social issue by every means available.

This focusing on some major evil has, in my opinion, helped to alleviate that evil. People seldom change until they are forced to see that a certain practice is wrong.

For instance, there is no doubt in my mind that the tremendous emphasis of the church during the sixties on justice for blacks was a major factor in bringing what progress there has been in the church, even though this emphasis led to exaggerations, bitterness, and splintering.

But the problem is: Which evil will be picked out as the crucial one while the rest are ignored? Which one will be made the test of whether a person is a Christian or not? The black person who has suffered greatly from a lack of justice, caused by people who consider themselves good Christians, might understandably want to make this a test of whether a person is really sincere.

A person who has been scarred by some other unfairness might also want to make that the test. For instance, suppose a person has had his life crushed by adultery—humiliated by the deceit and the betrayal, called to be father of someone else's child—and is trying to be like Hosea. He might very well want to make this the test, bitterly resenting the jolly-good-time-for-everyone attitude that seems to prevail. He might very much want a rule that people stop hopping from bed to bed or get out of the church. Often a person wants to build the test around the evil that has hurt him the most.

Picking out certain key evils runs into some other problems. Over a period of time, what was once a significant issue becomes a dry husk. This has certainly become true of the traditional attitude toward the use of liquor. Not only dry husks, but also a cheap way to get a sense of salvation. I remember some comments that Kenneth Foreman, my theology professor in seminary, made. He pointed out that the use of liquor was not a problem for him. He could pass a bar without even a thought of going in. Why should he take pride in not drinking when it was no temptation? But there were temptations that he had to wrestle with. Usually a person wants the rules set so that the key sins are not the ones that tempt him. If he can easily conform, then he has a mechanism for escaping the predicament—"Jesus is really on my side because I don't do those things."

Even if rules could be agreed upon, how would people be judged? For instance, take the integration of schools through the transferring of pupils from one school to another. Is the person who lives in a suburb that is unaffected by such transfers, but who advocates them, meeting the rule? I remember a few years ago when there was a dispute in Syracuse over transfers. A number of church executives took a position on it, criticizing those who were opposed to this practice. A church member who lived in an integrated neighborhood, but who was opposed to the transfers, angrily told me, "I'm getting tired of you preachers who live in the suburbs shooting your mouths off about what ought to be done in Syracuse. I live in an integrated neighborhood. We have tried to make it work, but these transfers are destroying everything we've worked for. If you guys want to solve the problems of Syracuse, why don't you live where I live?"

Suppose a decision is made to transfer students between Fayetteville (where I live) and Syracuse. If I were to oppose that, I would be condemned. But many people would say that it was a personal decision if I decided to send my kids to a private school because of the low quality of the public schools in Syracuse. But really, what is the difference?

I suppose that making rules and trying to get church members to shape up or else will never cease to attract people who will see this as the way to usher in a new golden era in the church. But it is a mirage that disappears when reached for. The attempt always ends in the grinding down of the gospel, a turning of it into dry husks, that neither offer hope nor encourage people to grow as Christians. It always becomes a mechanism by which to escape the predicament.

The problem of how to decide who is abiding by the rules has led people to set standards which make it possible to measure the degree of conformity. Protestants have long criticized Roman Catholics for their use of the sacraments that way—a person thinking he is a good Catholic because he goes to Mass every week, goes to confession when he is supposed to, takes Communion regularly, and always utilizes the other sacraments of the church when appropriate. Many Roman Catholics recognize that their sacramental system is susceptible to abuse. But they have no monopoly on the abuse of sacraments. Protestants often have their "sacraments" that can be used to prove that they measure up.

One of the most popular Protestant "sacraments" is the proper stance, or the use of the right words. My first exposure to this was in southern Indiana. Some church members were addicted to the use of certain phrases such as "We are saved by the blood of the cross." No matter how well a minister tied his sermon to the Bible, if he did not use those pat phrases, these church members were convinced that he was not really preaching the gospel.

Much to my amazement, I discovered a few years later that ministers can have the same addiction. In the spring of 1968, just after the Kerner Report was published, I heard a man speak on the crisis; one of the best speeches that I had heard. Yet, a couple of ministers grumbled afterward about the irrelevancy of the speech. Why hadn't the speaker dealt with the crisis of the moment? It was only after I had thought about the speech for several weeks that I realized why they thought the speech was irrelevant. Not once had the speaker used *racism* or *urban crisis.* I soon discovered that in the excitement of that spring a person could talk about anything and be considered relevant as long as he began with, "In light of the urban crisis . . ."

The more I observed speeches and actions, the more I came to see how important the proper stance was. A few years ago it became quite popular to condemn the so-called edifice complex. If a person said some good things about church building, there were always those who would condemn him for being more interested in buildings than people. But a church executive could condemn our obsession with buildings and many people would be convinced that the executive really had the priorities straight, even if he encouraged every small congregation in every overchurched village to add on, renovate, or build. His actions could be ignored; it was his words that counted. And I could cite a couple of dozen other examples. The proper stance, the right words spoken at the proper time, proved that he was a good Christian, no matter what his actions or private reservations.

Most of the efforts to escape the predicament seek a way to prove that a person is really doing Jesus's will, that he is acting in a way that Jesus approves.

77

But some people in the church through the centuries have tried to escape the predicament by saying that what one does doesn't matter. It's all a matter of inner feeling. If one has Jesus in his heart, he can do as he pleases. There is even a fancy word for it, antinomianism. While it has had a variety of shapes and sizes, the basic concept has been that ethical conduct is unimportant. Its basic argument has been that since it is impossible to always act morally, and in fact most people do fall far short of the moral ideal, why try to achieve the impossible and feel guilty about one's failures; instead just do what one pleases and enjoy life. Since sex is one of people's biggest problems, antinomianism has often endorsed casual sexual relations, one partner today and another tomorrow.

While there are many people who would say that a lot of church members are practicing antinomianists —church on Sunday to pray to God and the rest of the week prey on others—it has never really caught on in the church, and for a good reason. A sense of right and wrong, a sense that one ought to act in a certain way, is built into most people.

Even a man like D. H. Lawrence, in spite of the fact that many people think his ideas about sex are immoral, did not believe in antinomianism. He sought a way to build a just world. He was embittered and disillusioned by what industrialization had done to the world. England had been debauched by machine, factory, and mine. Where once there had been beauty, there was now hideousness. People were degraded by industrialization, turned into tools to be used until they wore out and then tossed aside. Then there was

World War I. All the industrial progress, the technical achievements, and the cultural attainments had not kept all hell from breaking loose in Europe; rather these had made things worse. Society was bankrupt and the two biggest symbols of that bankruptcy were education and religion. Mankind was consumed by injustice and was on the road to disaster.

Why was all this true? And what could be done about it? In Lawrence's mind the world was hell because people had forgotten what they were—talking animals. Lawrence did not mean animal in a bad sense. Consider for a moment the coyote. Coyotes mate for life, are good parents, and seem to live happily—which is a lot more than can be said for many people. They are not encumbered by all the paraphernalia of society. Their lives are based on a natural sexual attraction between a male and a female. Here, Lawrence saw the hope of the world—strip away all the phoniness of civilization and let people be free to be what they were meant to be by nature; let sex be free to unite people on the basis of its natural attraction. Meaningful relationships would be established, people would find happiness, and justice would flood the world. At this point I don't want to get bogged down in the practicality of what he suggested or whether it was actually a way of salvation, which I don't believe it was. I only want to show that Lawrence, who rejected much of our conventional morality, was not an advocate of antinomianism. Lawrence's goal was not a world where everyone would do as he pleased which for Lawrence would have been a continuation of the hell he detested, but a world in which people would do justice and love kindness.

Antinomianism—lawlessness—has seldom been seen as a solution to the predicament. In fact people are usually more fearful of lawlessness than they are of hypocrisy—pretending that a person is doing Jesus' will when he isn't. Many people have felt that every defense possible must be erected against the threat of lawlessness. As we have come to realize in recent years, most people seem to cherish law and order more than freedom, or almost anything else. It is not surprising then that the church, made up of people as it is, has traditionally been attracted to law and order.

If people must choose between lawlessness and hypocrisy, they choose hypocrisy. Many people have not seen how one can live honestly with the predicament, firmly grasping the need and the failure to be faithful. How can Jesus both accept our failures and call us to do his will? How can a person say that it's OK to fail and yet be motivated to do what is right, or at least try?

It is necessary to keep in mind this excessive fear of lawlessness in order to understand why the church has created so many mechanisms by which to escape the predicament, and why the church most of the time has not been happy with Paul and his views. In fact, Paul has been the most praised yet ignored writer in the New Testament—like a house revolutionary, nice to have around but let's not get carried away with his wild ideas.

The church may give lip service to Paul's righteousness through faith, but it doesn't usually buy it. Or if it does, it aims to buttress it with plenty of law and order. It's not going to risk everything by depending on it. And its fears are not without foundation. The writer of James was upset because people tried to use Paul's views to excuse their unchristian actions.

What does it profit, my brethren, if a man says he has faith but has not works? Can his faith save him? If a brother or sister is ill-clad and in lack of daily food, and one of you says to them, "Go in peace, be warmed and filled," without giving them the things needed for the body, what does it profit? So faith by itself, if it has no works, is dead.

But some one will say, "You have faith and I have works." Show me your faith apart from your works, and I by my works will show you my faith. . . . Do you want to be shown, you shallow man, that faith apart from works is barren? Was not Abraham our father justified by works, when he offered his son Isaac on the altar? (2:14-18, 20-21).

The writer was so upset that he tried to refute Paul's claim that one is justified by faith. While Paul argued that Abraham was justified by faith, the writer of James argued that Abraham was justified by works.

Paul's views, with a little twisting here and there, have made a handy hook for antinomianism, which has probably done more damage to Paul than anything else. Even Paul seems to have had trouble with that, or at least his letters to the Corinthians indicate such. Some people in the church there seemed to think that since they were saved, anything went—even getting drunk and having a fight during communion.

It has seldom been enough, then, for the church to

try to live by the belief that, because Jesus has made us his friends we are right with God, that we can live both as those who are unfaithful and those who are trying to be faithful, and that we don't have to play games with Jesus—pretending a loyalty that isn't. The church by and large flees the predicament. It rejects the fact that a person can't be a Christian in an imperfect world, and to cover up its rejection of reality, it plays games—nostalgia for the persecuted church, becoming a professional Christian, making some rules, or reducing Christianity to some proper practices. In its fears it cannot admit that a person can be both an SOB and a friend of Jesus, because it cannot believe that admitting that is the way to anything but disaster. I can understand the church's fears. I can understand why so many church members are unable to be honest with themselves. But I cannot play the games any more. I will live within the predicament—trying to hold firm to the fact that I am unfaithful and also to the fact that Jesus has called me to faithfulness.

6.

A Wordly Man's Approach to Jesus

I left two questions unanswered in the last chapter. How does a person live honestly with the fact that there is a gap between what he is and what Jesus wants him to be? And, how can the gospel so enter a person's life that he changes and grows, decreasing the gap between him and Jesus? The first has to do with the ever-present moment. The second has to do with what happens to a person over a length of time. I want to deal with the first question in this chapter and the next, and the second question in chapter 8.

My answer begins with the friendship between Jesus and a person. I touched on that in the chapter, "If We Didn't Have Jesus, We'd Have to Invent Him." I see this friendship with Jesus as the key to it all. Jesus wants to be my friend and he has invited me to be his. What brings us together then is the bond of friendship.

Such a friendship must be built on honesty. I am what I am and he is what he is. I can't pretend that I am something other than what I really am and Jesus won't. While most of the friendships that a person has with other people depend on each one living up to the expectations of that friendship, this is not true of a friendship between Jesus and a person. While someone may say, "Well, so-and-so was my friend once but he let me down," Jesus never says that. In fact, if Jesus had that view of friendship, he wouldn't be a friend to any of us very long.

A good illustration of Jesus' kind of friendship is the one that he had with Peter.

One day Jesus and his disciples were discussing who people were saying he was. Finally Jesus asked, "But who do you say that I am?"

Peter answered, "You are the Christ." Jesus was pleased with Peter's answer.

Then Jesus began to tell them that he would be killed. This upset Peter and he tried to get Jesus to stop talking such nonsense. But Jesus, quick as a flash, turned on Peter and shut him up. "Get out of my sight, you're helping the devil. You're not on God's side, you're on man's."

Peter said what he thought, Jesus said what he thought—and neither went off in a huff.

On the night before Jesus was killed, he told the disciples that they would all flee when he was arrested.

"Not me," piped up Peter. "The rest may run like scared rabbits, but I won't."

"Who are you trying to kid?" Jesus wanted to know. "Before the sun gets over the horizon, you

84

will have sworn up and down that you don't know me."

And sure enough, most of them fled and Peter denied Jesus. In fact he got so scared that he blurted out, "Damn it, I don't know the guy," or words like that. With friends like that, who needs enemies?

Most of us would have had our bellies full by that time. But not Jesus. After the resurrection, Jesus made a special point of assuring Peter that they were still friends.

Now a big production has been made out of how much Peter changed after the resurrection. Phooey! The fact of the matter is that Peter was just as capable of being an SOB after the resurrection as he was before. Paul and Peter got into it one time over eating with Gentiles. There was a group in the church that was finicky about eating with Gentiles. They weren't going to eat with Gentiles unless those Gentiles conformed to all the rules of Judaism. At first Peter wouldn't have any of that nonsense, but he let some people scare him into going along. Paul wrote in Galatians that he had to stand up to Peter and make him back off. And what would have happened to Jesus' movement, if the people in the church started treating the Gentiles like second-class citizens. It would probably have wandered off into the mist of history. But still Jesus didn't have his belly full. He went on being Peter's friend and wanting Peter to be his. If Peter ever fully lived up to Jesus' friendship, it was at the moment of death.

Jesus is the one who seeks friendship. I, or anyone, respond because I know that Jesus cares about people.

Jesus showed that he cared by dying on the cross. It didn't do him any good but it does us a lot of good. As Paul pointed out, when a person is willing to die for someone else, there isn't any doubt about that person's caring for others. Also as Paul pointed out, one doesn't run across a person being willing to die for someone else very often.

I remember reading during the Korean War about a misfit inductee. He soon became the butt of all the jokes in his training platoon. The sergeant, a veteran of the war, soon became disgusted with this useless excuse for a soldier and made his life hell. One day the men in his platoon decided to play a clever joke on him. A dummy grenade was obtained. The sergeant told the platoon that it was a live grenade. He handed it to one of the inductees to throw. The inductee pulled the pin and fumbled with it, letting it drop at the feet of the misfit. Quick as a flash the misfit fell on the grenade, burying it in his stomach. As the seconds ticked by, he slowly realized that it was all a joke. He had made an ass of himself again. In humiliation he finally looked up. But no one was laughing. The sergeant slowly helped the misfit to his feet and carefully dusted him off. Never again did anyone laugh at the misfit's bumbling. The fool was willing to die for those who ridiculed him. Jesus was like that.

Jesus, from the very beginning, showed how much he cared about people. The Gospels are overrun with incidents. He went to Jericho and had lunch with Zacchaeus. A lot of people were mightily upset at the idea of Jesus actually having lunch with such. Another time Jesus was having lunch with a Pharisee. A prosti-

tute snuck in and began to kiss Jesus' feet. The Pharisee thought he had been took by Jesus because he
didn't kick the prostitute away.

I have the feeling that we have read those incidents
so often that we have lost the disturbing sense of what
Jesus did. It was like Jesus going to Washington and
inviting the people who broke into the Watergate to
have lunch with him, or inviting one of the groups
who burned draft records to have lunch with him.
Jesus, being Jesus, would have lunch one day with
the Watergate gang and the next with the draft records burning gang. That is, he would if they would
be willing to have lunch with him. (And this is important. I don't plan to dwell on it, but it takes two to
have a friendship. No matter how much Jesus may
want to be friendly, he is just wasting his time if a
person doesn't want Jesus for a friend.)

As I have pointed out before, it sometimes seems to
me that God's trying to deal with the world on the
basis of Jesus being friends of people is a heck of a way
to try to run a world. With the kind of friends that
Jesus has, the kind most of us are, it's no wonder that
the world is in a mess. I suppose that from God's
point of view, the whole business is a real pain in the
neck. However, God seems to be behind the eight
ball. This seems to be the only game plan that may
work. God has to work with people where they are
and encourage them to become something better.
To threaten or to punish fails—people cannot be
scared into doing God's will. Destruction ends the
whole effort. And, evidently God has not given up on
people yet.

My statement about friendship with Jesus being the only game plan that may work is based on my understanding of Jesus' temptation experience. How could he get people to do God's will? This seems to be the basic question that he was wrestling with. Not by razzle-dazzle, not by naked power, but by friendship was the answer that he found.

(I cannot help wondering if God realized the mess he was getting into when he created people.)

Honesty requires me to face very frankly the fact that I am called to be a part of the world and also to be a follower of Jesus. There is a tension between these, points of conflict. I don't want to get involved with the question of just how evil the world is. It is enough to say that the world as it is is not an ideal world. There are points where I must choose between what the world wants me to do and what Jesus wants. (While there have been church members who have taken the position that the world and Jesus are in harmony, most church members would agree with me that there are times when one must choose.)

Which shall come first, then—the world or Jesus? A lot of people would immediately answer, "Jesus, of course." However, I would answer, "The world, of course." Now before someone has a fit and falls through it, let me explain why my answer is the opposite of the usual one.

I think it is time that we looked honestly at the problem and stopped glibly mouthing pat answers that don't really mean a thing. Sure I can sing in church every Sunday, "I'll follow Jesus wherever he wants me to go." I can loudly proclaim to all that

I'm going to put Jesus first. I'm not talking about what any one of us might tell others; I'm talking about the decisions that we really make—the choices that count, not the blah-blah that we may peddle.

Let me try to make as clear as possible the issue that confronts each of us. Each person is a part of the world, and he has to take that fact seriously. If a person is to be a friend of Jesus, he has to take that fact seriously. To say that the world comes first is not the same as saying that Jesus is irrelevant or merely kicking him aside as useless. It is to say that there are those points where I will be loyal to the world and not to Jesus. In popular terminology, we might say, we are faced with two top priorities, Jesus and the world. Which will be number one and which number two? I'm just saying that the world is priority one and Jesus priority two.

When we look back across the history of the church, we discover that the responses that members have made to the question of which comes first can be generally grouped into two categories. Ernst Troeltsch, in his book *The Social Teaching of the Christian Church,* calls one of these categories the sect-type response and the other the church-type response. I think it would be better to describe these as the absolute-loyalty-to-Jesus response and the responsible-participation-in-the-social-order response, which I will call the responsible-participation response.

The absolute-loyalty-to-Jesus response seeks to put Jesus first in every situation. Whenever there is a conflict, whatever stands between the person and Jesus must go. The responsible-participation response will endeavor to do what Jesus wants, but when there are conflicts it will often be necessary for Jesus to take second place.

It is always easy to condemn the idea of letting Jesus take second place without facing up to the problem involved. Many people lament the fact that the church is corrupted by the world. They yearn for a return to the early church when the theme song of its members seemed to be, "Follow Jesus and to hell with Rome." Then came the acceptance of Christianity as the official religion of the empire and the church went down the drain.

Ernst Troeltsch, after a careful study of church history, rejected as a myth the above view of the history of the church, and I think that he was right. It was his judgment that both responses, absolute loyalty to Jesus and responsible participation, were valid. A church member could in good conscience, so to speak, follow either one. He showed that both of these could be traced back to the New Testament—the absolute-loyalty-to-Jesus response to the teachings of Jesus, and the responsible-participation response to Paul. He then pointed out that both these responses are necessary if Jesus is to influence the world. While the person who seeks to be absolutely loyal to Jesus will usually in his personal actions and thoughts be much closer to what Jesus wants than the responsible participator, he seldom is able to directly influence the world. His absolute loyalty presents the Christian ideal to the world, but it is usually an ideal that strikes most people as impossible of realization. The person who seeks to be a responsible participant in the social

90

order usually acts and thinks in a way that gives a cloudy witness of Jesus' will, but he does have a greater opportunity to influence and change the social order. Troeltsch concluded that it was those church members who, having been responsible participants and sensitized by the absolute loyalists, had been able to improve the social order.

If the church just crawls in bed with the social order, it will be ineffective in improving society. If the church is just a persecuted, laughed at, or ignored minority on the fringe of society, it will also be in-effective in improving society. It is important to keep in mind that ineffectiveness is just that, whether it comes from the one or the other. And being effective is the purpose of it all. I do not believe in a faith by which I am saved, that says, "Let the rest of the world go to hell." I wish that those who yearn for the time when church members put Jesus first and to hell with Rome would realize that they are always in dan-ger of falling into the trap of, "I'm saved, and that's all that counts."

Neither the absolute loyalist nor the responsible participant ought to climb on any moral high horse and think that he has a monopoly on Jesus. As I have already argued, even the most dedicated church mem-ber has at least one blind spot, one place where his life is radically out of step with what Jesus wants. While the most dedicated person, the absolute loyalist, may live a life that more fully reflects the will of Christ than the rest of us, that is not the same as being perfect. The person who robs a bank cannot escape prosecution by arguing that he faithfully obeys all

91

other laws, so his bank robbing should be overlooked. While the responsible participant may pride himself on the fact that he wrestles with the problems of life by being part of the workaday world, he all too easily ignores Jesus.

When we move from trying to summarize in a systematic way these two responses to the ways these responses work themselves out in the lives of people, the situation becomes more complex. It is true that Paul's understanding of the Christian faith did lay the foundation for the responsible-participation response to Jesus. Paul's attitude toward the government did encourage an overlooking of evil—for example, slavery as a social arrangement. Yet when push came to shove, he was willing to die for Jesus. Some others— such as James, Jesus' half-brother—who were equally willing to die for Jesus and disagreed with Paul's assessment of the governing authorities advocated things such as full conformity to Jewish customs that could have led the church down a dead-end street. One can point to responsible participants who, because of their friendship to Jesus, greatly improved the moral level of society, and to absolute loyalists who went off into the desert to gaze at their navels.

I hope that my explanation will help you understand my comment of "the world, of course" having priority, and also will help you see the choice that faces each church member. Which response to Jesus will he choose, absolute loyalty or responsible participation?

I have, like everyone else, one free choice. By free I am not talking about whether a person is really free to choose between alternatives or whether his choices are determined—the whole question of whether there is such a thing as free will. By free I am referring to the fact that I can make one choice that is not contingent on other choices. Once I have used that one free choice, everything else is contingent on it. If this isn't clear, I aim to make it clear before I am done.

When Jesus confronted me as someone with whom I wanted to develop a friendship, I had to choose the kind of response I would make to Jesus. Would it be the absolute-loyalty response or the responsible-participation response? I thought that I was making the absolute-loyalty response, but I wasn't. I thought that it was a mental choice to be implemented by the earnestness of my feelings at the moment and the power of will. What I failed to see at that point was that choice was not made by a mental decision; it was made on the basis of the decisions I made about my life. I decided to become a minister in the Presbyterian Church, U.S.A. and a pastor. By that decision I had chosen the responsible-participation response. My decisions since then have reaffirmed that initial decision. I became a church bureaucrat. I own a house in a suburb. I enjoy the benefits of affluency. More than that, I am a white male in a society organized to give educated white males the greatest advantage. Along the way I have made the necessary compromises to be effective in the pattern of life that I have chosen and to maintain my place in it.

In the process, I have undertaken a variety of obligations. I have a mortgage to pay as well as other bills.

93

I have a family to support. If I don't make the welfare of my children of first importance, no one, except my wife, will. I have a job to do as a church executive. All this presses in upon me, forcing me from time to time to compromise my Christian convictions.

Given the decisions I have made and the situation in which I find myself, if I am to be a follower of Jesus, it has to be on the basis of the responsible-participation-in-the-social-order response. To pretend that I have made or can make the absolute-loyalty-to-Jesus response would be like a prostitute pretending that she was a virgin. Further, if Jesus is going to get any good out of me, it has to be on the basis of my being a part of the society. I don't see how I can be of help to Jesus pretending that I am something I'm not.

If I were to decide to change my response to the absolute-loyalty-to-Jesus response, more is required than a mental decision. I would have to significantly change my pattern of life. I will pick up on that in a bit when I discuss the absolute-loyalty response.

I want to make clear at this point the fact that compromise is an essential component of the responsible-participation response. Suppose a person who wants to be a follower of Jesus decides to become a politician—a very honorable occupation (my second choice as a career). By becoming a politician he has used up his one free choice. All other decisions, including his response to Jesus, must be contingent on his free choice. Compromise is an essential component of being a politician—and condemning politicians for compromising is like condemning a bus driver for driving a bus. If a politician is to make a useful contribution to the political process, he must be continually engaged in compromise. He will find himself supporting as good what, from his understanding of Jesus' will, is not good. By becoming a politician, the follower of Jesus becomes part of a system that has much wrong with it, and at times he must support the wrongness, or at least keep his mouth shut about it.

I cannot deal in detail with the problem of compromise. It is the unexplored problem in the church. Like sex in times past, we don't talk about it. But before moving on, I would like to make four brief comments. To deny the reality of compromise is not to end it, but to drive it underground where people cannot honestly deal with it. Compromise should always be with a purpose, to gain something tomorrow by giving up something today, or to gain half a loaf instead of no loaf. Even though it can be defended on the basis of gaining as well as losing, one should still keep in mind that compromise puts Jesus in second place. There is a limit to compromise, a point beyond which a person destroys whatever integrity he has.

Coupled with the need to compromise is the problem of making decisions in the real world. In life, most decisions are a choice between alternatives, not absolutes. The person who assumes responsibility in the social order is not always free to follow what he perceives to be Jesus' will. He is often forced to choose between alternatives, both of which are an affront to Jesus.

Let me go back and pick up again two ideas—the one free choice and the absolute-loyalty-to-Jesus response. When a person uses his one free choice to make an absolute-loyalty-to-Jesus response, he then makes every other decision contingent on that. The pattern of his life reflects his one free choice decision. In order to illustrate that, I want to turn to the Roman Catholic branch of the church and its religious orders. It seems to me that the religious orders have on the whole, much more so than Protestantism, understood the fact that the absolute-loyalty response requires a pattern of life in harmony with that decision. The writer of II Timothy put his finger on this when he wrote, "Share in suffering as a good soldier of Christ Jesus. No soldier on service gets entangled in civilian pursuits, since his aim is to satisfy the one who enlisted him" (2:3-4).

A good illustration of this is St. Francis of Assisi. His father was a well-to-do merchant and Francis benefited from his father's wealth. As a young man he led a carefree, playboy life. He joined the army and was captured. After he spent a year as a prisoner of war, his outlook toward life began to change. He spent a great deal of time by himself seeking God's will. When Francis made the decision to become an absolutely loyal follower of Jesus, he began to pattern his life accordingly. He gave up his carefree, playboy ways and began to nurse the sick. He begged for the poor. He sold his fine clothes, and also some merchandise from his father's store, to raise money so a priest could rebuild a ruined church. When this brought him into conflict with his father, Francis renounced his inheritance, even taking off the clothes his father had given him. St. Francis was going to be a soldier of Jesus and not get entangled in civilian pursuits that would come between him and Jesus.

In using St. Francis as an illustration, I am not necessarily arguing that his style of life was the right one. The point is, having made his decisions he sought a life-style compatible with them. When he had to choose between his understanding of what it meant to be loyal to Jesus and what the world required, the world had to give way. He did not see how he could be absolutely loyal to Jesus and be part and parcel of a wealthy minority in a sea of poverty.

It is not surprising that the absolute-loyalty response within Protestantism has been confined to groups made up of poor people outside the mainstream. Nor is it surprising that when the members of such a group moved into the mainstream of society the absolute-loyalty response was replaced by the responsible-participation response. The change was necessitated by a change in situation. Recently the *Wall Street Journal* had an article on young activists who had been elected to public office. The change in situation required a change in the way they dealt with issues. As one said, "I've learned that to get along I have to go along." He had to learn how to be a good politician. Each of them was worried about losing his ideals, but each saw that he could only achieve them through the process of compromise. In the campaign of 1972, a young liberal legislator running for his second term was asked what he had learned. "I have learned that in politics it is a choice between alternatives, not between absolutes."

Neither is it surprising that what Troeltsch called

the church-type and I call the responsible-participation response can be traced back to Paul, and what Troeltsch called the sect-type and I call the absolute-loyalty response can be traced back to Jesus and his Palestinian disciples. Paul was a Roman citizen, part of the established social order. Jesus and his disciples were a subject people, shut out from the established social order.

The refusal to face and accept the fact that a person cannot be both a full participant in the social order and absolutely loyal to Jesus has led to all kinds of nonsense and deceptions. For instance, the nonsense that ministers should be prophets. The idea that every preacher should be a prophet is ridiculous. Any thoughtful look at the Old Testament should have made clear that prophets are few and far between. Depending on how one divides up the material, no more than twenty prophets made it into the Old Testament and some of them had their names forgotten. If one is quite conservative in the period covered, say four hundred years, one of these came along about every twenty years. On top of that most of the guys who ran around claiming to be prophets got put down as false prophets. Amos rejected the idea that he was a prophet because he held them in such ill repute. One can only wonder with amazed cynicism how the idea ever got abroad that every preacher could have a hot line to God. Instead of every preacher being an eager beaver about being a prophet, he ought to be scared to think he was.

This silly idea that preachers are prophets has become a license for them to use so-called prophetic preaching as a guilt-unloading mechanism. By playing prophet and condemning people, a minister can cover up his inability to deal with the discrepancy between his personal desires and being loyal to Jesus. For instance, there was a young man in his first pastorate who, having been flimflammed by all this nonsense, tried to play prophet in the pulpit. Anyone who disagreed with his views on the social issues was put down as being out of step with Jesus.

The congregation that he had been called to serve owned an old manse in the center of the small village. Prior to his coming the congregation completely redecorated and renovated the manse so it would be an adequate and comfortable home for the new pastor. It was not a new house and it was not in the fancy subdivision at the edge of the village. He pestered the congregation until it built a new house in that subdivision.

It is understandable how a young man raised in an affluent society would place such high value on a fine house in the right part of town, that he would desire it so much that he was willing to place a heavy burden on a small congregation, a burden that would force them to divert money from mission giving. I understand that and am willing to be tolerant of it. But it undermines his claim to be a prophet. What is much worse, the idea that he is in some special position to tell others exactly what the Lord requires becomes a falsehood.

If old Amos came back and if he had a sense of humor, he would find hilariously funny the idea that ministers who follow every zig-zag of fashion, who have to have a house as fine as the best, and who have both front feet firmly planted in the trough of affluency consider themselves twentieth century versions of Old Testament prophets.

No wonder the church is in a mess. Look what all this does to ministers. They are constantly pressured into being false persons, trying to be what they can't be. The marvel of it is that we don't have more mental basket cases in the ministry. A good front is better than being honest—which seemed to be the idea in the Watergate cover-up.

(I don't mean by my comments that ministers shouldn't seek prophetic insight to understand the Lord's will for this day. But there is an awful lot of difference between humbly trying to discover the Lord's will as one who is also a sinner and arrogantly proclaiming what the Lord's will is as though one had a hot-line to heaven.)

I refuse to play the popular games. I am no prophet. I am not St. Francis. I am a worldly man, and I must approach Jesus on that basis. Amid the pressures of this life I seek to do his will, knowing full well the persistency of my failures and the frequency of my putting him in second place. I am of the world. He is not. There is a gulf fixed between us. The bridge is his hand reaching out to me in friendship. I want that friendship, but it must be a friendship based on honesty.

7.

Putting Jesus in His Place

It's time we put Jesus in his place. And his place is over against us. In many ways Jesus is our enemy, but not the normal kind. He is the friendly enemy—still he threatens us. He is the enemy of many of our values and actions. He is the friend who is also the enemy. Friend or foe becomes friend and foe in Jesus.

How can that be? We have friends and we have enemies. Friends are for us and enemies are against us. How can we speak of Jesus being both friend and enemy at the same time? How can he be both for and against us? How can he who comes to us as friend also come to us as enemy?

I have no simple answers to those questions. But, part of the answer is that I am both friend and enemy of Jesus. I am his enemy whenever I block him in this world. When Peter objected to Jesus talking about his being killed, Jesus said to him, "Get behind me, Satan! For you are not on the side of God, but of men" (Matthew 8:33). Jesus' response could be paraphrased, "Get out of my way, enemy."

If Jesus really cares about us, he must come as enemy as well as friend. I think that we can see this by turning to the relationships between people. In the long run, is not the best friend the one who comes as enemy too? Kaiser Wilhelm II resented Metternich, who was his ambassador to England shortly before World War I. One of Metternich's reports on a proposal made by Lloyd George, then Chancellor of the Exchequer, made the Kaiser so furious that he wrote on it, "One of these days he must give those gentlemen who object to our 'wanton aggressive ambitions' a coarse answer like, 'Kiss my ass,' to knock a little sense into their heads. Metternich ought to get a good kick in his behind. He is too soft."

Very calmly, Metternich wrote in response, "I should be falsifying history if I couched my reports otherwise. I cannot sell my convictions, not even for the favor of my sovereign. What is more, I doubt that I should be serving Your Majesty properly if I continued to send smooth reports until we suddenly found ourselves facing war with England."

Who was the real friend of the Kaiser, Metternich or the claque of flatterers with which the Kaiser surrounded himself?

Years ago an elder in one of the first churches I served told me of an incident that took place in the small rural community in which he lived. There was a man who for years had squabbled with everyone in the community, finding fault at every chance possible. The elder was president of the telephone co-op in the community. At one annual meeting, the obnoxious man was worse than usual. He made it almost impossible to carry on. Up to that point, everyone in the community had tried to overlook the man's insults and pacify him. The elder decided that enough was enough. He marched back to where the man was sitting. Pointing a finger at the man, the elder said, "Now, let me tell you something. You are the most obnoxious man I've ever met. All you do is make trouble and find fault. We're getting tired of it. If you can't act like a human being, why don't you stay home?"

The man was furious. He got up and stalked out of the meeting. The elder and everyone else wondered what the man would do. In a few weeks an amazing thing happened; the man completely changed. Gone were the angry faultfinding and troublemaking. In their place was a genuine effort to get along with people.

Some may object to my use of the word *enemy* to describe Jesus. I realize that my choice of the word can be criticized on the basis of some of the passages in the New Testament. However, my use is based on one of the attitudes that most people have. The average person divides people into friends and enemies. A person tends to react on the basis of whether another person is his friend or enemy. Whether my choice of the word is out of harmony with some passages in the New Testament I will not argue. However, it is certainly in harmony with human experience. It speaks to the situation.

I believe that most of us have become too buddy-buddy with Jesus. We try to get Jesus on our side. We try to wrap Jesus around whatever we believe or do. I sometimes feel that Jesus has become a sort of house pet to be trotted out at convenient points. Jesus is not the friend who is always on our side. He is the friend who is also our enemy.

I realize the danger of speaking of Jesus as an enemy. I certainly would not want to return to the view of God as an angry being, watching for the first chance to throw us into hell, with Jesus as his assistant. Every age has its problem with understanding God. Our problem, if I discern the situation correctly, is not that of making God a terrifying being, but of making him a domesticated creature. We do not need to come to see that God is love; we need to come to see that he is not in our hip pocket.

We cannot, I believe, ever talk about Jesus without remembering that he died for us. What he did shows us that he wants to be our friend. When I talk about Jesus as the enemy, I always speak of him as the enemy who died for us. If Jesus is the peculiar friend, he is also the peculiar enemy. I know of no other way to talk about Jesus than as both friend and foe.

The problem is that Jesus exceeds our capacity to understand him. In a sense he is the eternal mystery. For years scholars have debated whether a biography of Jesus can be written. Many scholars have argued that no biography can be written because our information is too fragmentary. I do not think that it could be done even if we had a transcript of every word spoken and deed done. Even then we would not fully understand Jesus. Jesus always confronts us as a riddle, but we can never solve it.

Life with Jesus is a predicament. I am supposed to be a follower of Jesus, but I live in a world where following him often seems to be impractical. I am to believe his words, but often I cannot agree with him. To honestly see myself as I am is to see myself as one who often disagrees with Jesus.

If I were to literally do some of the things that Jesus said, I am convinced that I would ruin my life. Jesus, as portrayed in the Gospels seemed to have a very irresponsible attitude toward the future as far as I am concerned—or at least the future in the kind of world in which we live. His ideas may have been fine for a basically agricultural, nonmoney society when people lived together in family groups spanning two or three generations. But we live in a money society, and it is essential that a person give very careful thought to the future.

Jesus told a parable about a wealthy man whose land was so productive that it was necessary for him to tear down his old barns and build new, larger ones. When the man saw all that he had, he decided to retire and enjoy himself. But God, according to Jesus, decided that that was the time for the man to die. The man was rich in goods, but poor toward God. Jesus then went on to tell his disciples not to be anxious about the necessities of life. God will provide.

As far as I am concerned a person must give very careful thought to his future and plan for retirement.

He must make it a major concern in his life. The rich man comes across to me as the prudent estate planner. It is my observation that ministers who are just busy serving God retire in poverty, while those who plan carefully for retirement and make the right decisions retire in comfort. God helps those who help themselves.

In the Sermon on the Mount, Jesus is quoted as saying, "But I say to you, Do not resist one who is evil. But if any one strikes you on the right cheek, turn to him the other also; and if any one would sue you and take your coat, let him have your cloak as well; and if any one forces you to go one mile, go with him two miles. Give to him who begs from you, and do not refuse him who would borrow from you" (Matthew 5:39-42).

In my judgment, if the practices of society followed Jesus' statements, the result would be chaos and the collapse of the social order. These statements would give license to every mentally disturbed, malicious, dishonest, or inconsiderate person to prey on others. The selfish strong would get all the good things and leave the crumbs to the weak. I believe that society must use force to restrain and remove those who will not follow the rules. I believe that a person becomes mature by learning that there are limits beyond which he cannot go; and if he does he will be hurt. I believe that we harm people by giving approval to conduct that is wrong. While I do not believe in malicious revenge, I do not believe in passive non-resistance either.

I sense over and over in the words of Jesus a threat

to my life-style. If I were to literally carry out some of his teachings, I would have to radically change. I see many of the goals in my life in direct opposition to my understanding of his teachings. Yet, I find meaning in my life-style. I do not want to give it up. Moreover, I do not see how I could survive, if I were to literally follow what he said. I would end up adrift on a stormy sea, finally to be wrecked on some alien coast.

Very frankly then, there is the point where Jesus becomes the enemy. I must resist him. When I read his teachings in the Gospels there are many times when I am convinced that they won't work, or they conflict so much with the way I do things that I just can't follow them, or I do not see them as practical for the kind of world in which I live, or I just don't understand what Jesus was driving at.

I can hear all kinds of reactions to what I have just written. I can hear someone say, "To admit what you have just admitted only proves that you are not really trying to be a Christian." Another voice is saying, "How dare you brush Jesus off as irrelevant?" Still another voice says, "You have misunderstood what Jesus meant."

Before anyone starts screaming and yelling too much, I would ask him to read carefully the Gospels. Let him measure his actions against Jesus' words. Let him show that he carries out all the teachings of Jesus. Take for instance Jesus' response to Peter's question about how many times he should forgive his brother. Jesus replied, "I do not say to you seven times, but seventy times seven" (Matthew 18:22). How many of us can literally carry that out?

When a person is confronted by his inability or unwillingness to literally carry out the teachings of Jesus, his response is often, "Well, you're not supposed to take them literally. Jesus was using exaggeration. He didn't mean it that way." All right, let's look at that a moment. Jesus told a parable about a man who went from Jerusalem to Jericho and on the way got beat up and robbed by a bunch of thugs. Jesus went on to point out that a priest and Levite just walked by, but a Samaritan stopped and helped the man. Now Jesus told the parable in response to a question about who is a person's neighbor.

Now suppose a "colored" family moved in next door to me. Someone might suggest that that parable had something to say to me about my relation to that "colored" family; such as, if they need help, I should help them. However, Jesus didn't mean it that-a-way, at all. Notice that in the parable the victim was a Jew and the two who passed by were Jews. Now the person who helped out was a Samaritan—and Jews and Samaritans hated each other. Jesus was saying, don't let a Samaritan show you up. To make that relevant to the present it must mean, if one of my white neighbors needs help, I shouldn't let that "colored" family show me up by being more helpful than I am.

I hope that it is obvious that I am exaggerating, but with a purpose in mind. I have gone out of my way in the last few paragraphs to put down the teachings of Jesus. Previously, I have argued that we have to take Jesus seriously. Jesus is hope and help to us. The responsible participant in the social order should try very hard to implement the teachings of Jesus because these lead to a world with greater justice. I realize that we often need to interpret Jesus' teachings, keeping in mind that he did use exaggeration. But my point is that there is a gap between Jesus and us, and we dare not lose sight of that. At some places we are in conflict with Jesus; he is the enemy.

For a person to deny the conflict between Jesus and himself is to enter into a falsehood, or to use a popular phrase, to engage in a cover-up. I am convinced that I must live in conflict with Jesus, a conflict for which I see no final solution in this life. Only by living in conflict with Jesus does the gospel have power in my life and in the world. I can see in my own life how, out of conflict with Jesus, what seemed irrelevant and impractical has become meaningful and practical.

Society has practices that are so ingrained that most people cannot see how it could function without them. The practices seem so necessary that most people see them as right, no matter how out of step with Jesus they are. I see a process at work. First of all, people begin to see that a particular practice is wrong. Then they suggest alternatives. Some people begin to follow a new practice. Finally society is moved to do away with the wrong practice. At each step Jesus is the enemy in conflict with society, calling it to be something different. If that conflict is covered up so that people no longer see it, the power of the gospel is gone. However, if Jesus is only seen as the enemy, then people will feel compelled to get him out of the way. If people are threatened too much by Jesus, they will only become more rigid. Jesus must not only be the enemy of society, he must also be the friend that leads society down a new path.

Jesus, in his place, is not only the friend who accepts and understands us; he is also the enemy in conflict with us.

8.

A Church for Sinners, Seekers, and Sundry Non-Saints

The ecclesiastical quality-control experts lament loud and long how we half-hearted Christians are screwing things up in the church.* We are the misfits in their kind of church. From their point of view, we are the despicable element in the church—and to make matters worse, we are the majority. They are sure that the church could accomplish marvelous things, if it weren't for us stragglers dragging our heels, wandering off, and sitting in the shade when it's time to march. They feel that the church has to spend so much time trying to nurse us along that it has scant energy left to change the world.

---

*I am using the word *church* in this chapter to mean the local church or congregation, the church as a collection of congregations, the church seen as a local organization of people.

And they are right. We are screwing up the church. Most of us are long-term loss propositions. Jesus won't get much production out of us. Maybe we ought to let the righteous have the church. I'm in favor of designing a church for us sinners, seekers, and sundry non-saints. Perhaps we ought not call it a church. We could call it the fellowship of failures, a place for people who have failed to set a good Christian example.

This would be a church for us who have seen Jesus from afar, but are so immersed in the world that we often lose sight of him in the pressure and whirl of living. We know that Jesus wants to be our friend, but we get so busy that we forget. We need a place where we can know Jesus as our friend. We need a place where we can be reminded over and over again that Jesus cares about us, because we do forget so easily. We need a place where we can be encouraged to try to do what Jesus asks. This would be a place for us basket-case church members.

My kind of church will not be a place for the righteous—not that I want to turn them away. They just won't be happy there. We'll have so many cripples that we'll be a terribly poor army. Perhaps we should rewrite "Onward, Christian Soldiers"—

> Onward, Christian soldiers,
> Hobbling as we go . . .

When I was in seminary, I heard about an ex-army officer who spoke one laymen's Sunday. He pointed out that church members liked to sing that hymn, which compares the church to an army. Then he pointed out the lackadaisical attitude that many people had about going to church. He wondered what kind of an army would one have, if soldiers only showed up for roll call when they were in the mood. He concluded by pointing out that, if the church really was an army, most of the church mmbers would be court-martialed. And he was right.

My kind of church will be about as far as one can get from a disciplined army. (In light of many people's attitude toward the army, they might want to shout, "Praise the Lord!" But I am not referring to the army in any derogatory way. In fact I am using the word in a very positive way, in terms of a disciplined group of people organized to accomplish a specific objective.) My kind of church in many ways will be a disaster. And the righteous just won't be happy there. The ecclesiastical quality-control experts will not be happy because the one thing we won't have is quality. The people who are absolutely sure of what God's will is, and that they are doing it, won't be happy because we'll be confused about what God's will is. Those who want to run around condemning people won't be happy because we'll not be in that business. "Dedicated" Christians would be better off going some place else.

The kind of people who will feel at home in my kind of church—a church for sinners, seekers, and sundry non-saints—are the people who have found something attractive about Jesus, but often have a meager friendship with him. It will be the home of the goofed-again people, people with a common sense

113

of their failure to act as Christians, people who realize that the best intentions on Sunday morning have often melted away by the afternoon. The people in my kind of church will be well aware of the fact that they do a poor job of setting an example for Jesus. They will come because they know that they need a lot of help if they're going to do anything that's Christian.

My kind of church will be a home for those who shouted, "Crucify him!" long ago. And we will know that if Jesus came back in the flesh and started causing a lot of trouble, we might again cry, "Crucify him!" We are the sinners who scorned Jesus that day, the sinners for whom he died.

My kind of church will be a place for people who want to consider whether some changes should be made in their lives. It won't be in the business of trying to force people to be this, that, or something else. Rather, it will seek to help them decide.

While my kind of church may very well attract people who will come for all kinds of reasons—it's the thing to do, there's nothing else to do on Sunday morning, or what better place is there to show off a new hat or suit—we will operate on the assumption that they come because they have some interest in Jesus, so we won't scream at them or condemn them for coming for the wrong reasons. We'll just be glad they came.

When I was a young pastor, I decided to see how many people I could find who were, in my judgment, mature Chrisians; so I made a mental list, a very short list for that matter. Over a few years, one by one, each of the persons on the list did something that I thought to be a major affront to Jesus. My list got shorter and shorter, until it was down to just two—my wife and me. Then I had to mark her off. In my loneliness I discovered that I had to mark myself off too. At that moment I realized that I had to accept everyone or no one—not even myself. I saw that the church had to make everyone welcome or no one. My kind of church will make everyone welcome.

My kind of church will let people be free to be themselves. People won't have to pretend that they are gung ho for Jesus if they're not. If they want to put on little masks so we won't know everything about them, that will be fine too. Honesty will be encouraged, but not demanded.

My kind of church will be different from the world —a place of shade from the world, a place of refreshment, a place to prepare people to return to the world, but above all a place where people don't have to fight the battles, a place of truce. People can meet there and discover their commonness amidst their differences. The mother whose son was killed in Vietnam can meet the mother whose son fled to Canada and share a common pain. The corporation executive can meet the assembly-line worker and discover their common interests. The black militant can meet the white racist and discover their common humanity. It will be a place of hope, that someday the peace discovered there will spread throughout the whole world.

Since my kind of church will recruit all us misfits, it will have to be designed with us in mind. It will have three basic tasks: the first task will be to help us cope with life, to know Jesus as friend; the second will be to help us develop a broader point of view, to live with Jesus-as-enemy; and the third task, to help us become responsible participants in the social order, to follow Jesus-as-leader.

The first task of my kind of church, then, will be to help people cope with life, to know Jesus-as-friend. It will exist first of all for those who are its members. I realize that there has been a great emphasis in recent years on the church existing for the world, not for itself. Theologians have argued that people are members of the church so that they can be sent out into the world to serve Jesus, not to be coddled. Many have condemned the average· congregation's preoccupation with its own members. Now perhaps a church for the righteous can concentrate on its mission to the world and play down the needs of its members. But my kind of church—for sinners, seekers, and sundry non-saints—must concentrate on its members. This may be a perversion of what the church ought to be, but when one is organizing a church for us who are the disreputable element, one has to design it to meet our needs.

I am not opposed to people organizing a church for the righteous, though I think a lot of them pretend to be more righteous than they really are. I want to organize a church for people for whom the heart is a disaster area—the woman rejected by a husband gallivanting around with his good-time girl, the man broken by the discovery of his wife's long-time affair, knowing not whether his children are his, the man haunted by the ghosts of far-off battlefields, the poverty-stricken teen-ager with everything that money will buy, except love, the parent embittered by a son's death in a resented war, the person cheated in life and emibttered because of the color of his skin. I want a church for people overwhelmed by life, not sure that the struggle is worth the effort.

If a person is going to cope effectively with life, he needs to find meaning for life, to be able to endure, to handle the crisis points, and to accept his temporality.

Life needs to make sense. Often underlying the search for meaning is the feeling that a person is a nonentity in a hostile and indifferent world. Who really cares whether he lives or dies? Jesus does. To discover that Jesus is seeking to be his friend is to discover that one is wanted.

Life often seems meaningless because a person experiences it as a maze of confusing information. While some of it suggests that life has meaning, much of the information suggests that life is useless and pointless. In Jesus' life in the flesh there is a clear witness to the meaning of life.

Almost every person at least once in his life does something that so wounds his conscience that self-respect is destroyed. How can he endure the shame of what he has done, face people who know? What he has done confirms the feeling of worthlessness. But Jesus, the friend of murderers, crooks, and prostitutes, seeks him out.

A person needs to be able to endure the corrosive forces in life, those things that would grind a person down so that he is reduced to pettiness and meanness, living life as a grudge against the world and

117

people in it. No one escapes injustice. While the poor and minorities are hounded by the injustices of life, even the wealthiest person can point to injustices done him. Seldom will a person reach the end of life without having been blasted by at least one senseless tragedy. Life sometimes seems to be filled with the pettiness of people. If the corrosive forces are not to grind a person down to bitterness, he needs Jesus' friendship as a shield and his life as an example.

Life is a series of crisis points, some part of the normal process of moving from babyhood to old age, and some only normal in the sense that everyone experiences some of them—accidents, sickness premature death, and sudden loss of a job. Each new crisis confronts a person with a new departure, a leaving behind of the old and the picking up of the new. Like the pilot taking a ship through a stormy channel to the open sea, a person must be able to navigate through each of these crises. Jesus is the pilot at these points.

Most people find it hard to accept the fact of temporality, that they must die. A person mentally has a grasp on eternity—he can learn about the distant past and imagine what the distant future may be like. He sees himself as a part of the procession of events, but he realizes that he is only a temporary part. In some way he must prepare himself to give up his place in the world. A person often finds himself caught between the feeling that life must reach beyond the grave and that death is the end. Jesus reminds us that life does extend beyond the grave.

118

I realize how easy it is for me to point to Jesus as the answer to each of these problems, and how difficult it is to discover him as the answer in actual experience. I realize that for many people Jesus is just a shadow far in the distance. Even for those of us who feel certain of our friendship with Jesus there are times, especially in times of crisis, when Jesus seems of no help.

Often in life we discover Jesus' friendship for us through the friendship of a person close at hand. My kind of church will be organized so that people can discover Jesus-as-friend in those around them. It will be organized to remind people over and over that Jesus is their friend and to reinforce their experience with him.

At the funeral home before my dad's funeral, one of his friends, Harold Lebbert, told me of the time that he and my dad were deer hunting on Rattle-snake Mountain and were still far from the car when it became dark. It was so dark that they had to hold their guns between them to be sure that they did not get separated. He told of the slow, stumbling journey to the car. Then he ended the story by saying, "I wasn't worried. If anyone could find his way off the mountain, it was your Dad. I knew that even if we had to spend the night on the mountain, we would be all right." Jesus is the friend who is with us in the darkness, and my kind of church will help people know Jesus as that kind of friend.

The second task of my church will be to help people to develop a broader point of view, to live with Jesus-as-enemy. I see this as an essential extension of the first task, helping people to cope with life. I believe that a person finds increasing meaning in life as he is freed from his fears, prejudices, and blindness. I also believe that a person gains his freedom from these in the experience of confrontation. If Jesus is to help a person, Jesus must confront him as enemy. The person must see himself as he really is, he must see Jesus as over against him, and he must try to see the world as Jesus sees it.

Often a person's fears, prejudices, and blindness are built on myths. A person fears what he does not know. The stranger is always one to be viewed with suspicion. The natural tendency is to be fearful of those who have different life-styles, skin colors, and social standing. Prejudice seems to be almost universal. Almost everyone has a group that he looks down upon, that he scorns, and that he dismisses as of no value. For instance, while many well-educated people condemn others for their prejudices against other races, many of these same well-educated people can be just as prejudiced against hard hat workers. I have already made much ado of blindness in the earlier chapters of the book, so I do not need to add anything more at this point.

Each fear, prejudice, and blindness is often built on myths—views of people and the world that don't fit the facts. Each of these causes a person to feel threatened. Each is a threat leading to helplessness because a person is trying to deal with what is not real and, in the case of blindness, to perpetuate the very kinds of injustice that a person dislikes. A person needs a more realistic appraisal of the world, to see it and the people in it as they are.

I am not suggesting that a realistic appraisal will lead to a removal of all differences between people or suddenly usher in a period of universal justice. Some fears are based on reality. There are times when a person discovers that no matter how good his intentions or how strong his desire for friendship, others will continue to try to do him harm. A person may dislike some people with good reason. Justice is often the balancing of conflicting, but legitimate self-interests, more of a compromise than an agreed-upon universal principle of rightness. For instance, the farmer wants high prices for his crops so he can make a profit, and the consumer wants low prices for food so he can live within his income. Some differences are very real and create gaps between people. The person with a Ph.D. in literature will naturally feel more at home with someone who shares his interest in the classics than with a person who loves to read comic books.

Many experiences in life push us toward fear, prejudice, and blindness. For instance, on two occasions young men have stolen purses from the church center here in Syracuse. Having experienced that, a person finds it difficult, when he sees a poorly-dressed young man, not to be fearful and prejudiced and not to be indifferent to whether the police treat such people fairly or not.

But how is Jesus to confront a person as the enemy who challenges his fears, prejudices and blindnesses? How is one to know Jesus as the one calling him to learn to get along with others? It is so easy to have Jesus just as friend and to ignore him as enemy. The inevitable tendency is to see Jesus approving everything a person does. I have concluded that the vast majority of us will only be confronted by Jesus-as-enemy as we confront people who are different from us.

My church will be made up of diversity—of rich and poor, of young and old, of liberals and conservatives, of black and white. It will be a church searching for how to live diversely. I remember watching "All in the Family" one night. Archie and Mike (Meathead) were talking and arguing about the two years that Mike had lived there and reminiscing about his and Gloria's wedding. Finally Mike said to Archie, "You know, I think I've been good for you. You've mellowed a bit." I jumped up and shouted, "That's my kind of church!" My kind of church is where people can still live together in spite of their conflicts. It won't try to make anyone over, but hopefully each person will benefit from the insights of those with whom he disagrees, becoming less fearful, less prejudiced, and less blind. It will seek dialogue so that understanding and appreciation will increase and reconciliation take place.

Years ago, Yogi Berra and Bobby Brown both played for the New York Yankees and roomed together on the road. Yogi loved comic books and Bobby was studying to be a medical doctor. In the evening Yogi would read his comic books and Bobby his medical textbooks. One night Bobby slammed his book shut. "Well, how did it come out?" Yogi asked.

These two men were able to bridge the gap because they had baseball in common and had learned to appreciate each other. In my kind of church people will have Jesus in common and through him will learn to appreciate each other.

A few years ago I was involved in some slick ecclesiastical politicking, in fact I masterminded the thing. We defeated an incumbent judicatory officer who seemed to be safely entrenched. Being young I was quite proud of myself. A lot of people had written me off as a dumb hick and I had shown them who was dumb. Here I was, the young, rising church statesman (actually politician, but we don't like that word in the church) learning how to successfully manipulate the levers of power. Later that summer I had a chance to tell my brother Herb, who is a rural pastor, about it. I told the story in a way that would assure his being thoroughly impressed with his brother's genius. When I finished I leaned back in my chair to await his appropriate remark.

He looked at me for a moment, and then he said, "I don't want to make you mad, but I do have one question. How do you reconcile what you did with being a Christian?"

In my church a person will face that question quite often. In brotherly affection we will be Jesus-as-enemy to each other.

The third task of my kind of church will be to help people become responsible participants in the social order, to follow Jesus-as-leader. Again I see this as an essential extension of the first task, helping people cope with life. I believe that people find life meaningful as they are able to contribute to making the world run; they need to do more than just go along for the ride.

When I was a young pastor, one of the members of the congregation was a young man who had just gotten out of the navy. One day he told me about his experience in the service. Having gone into it from a rural area where he knew everyone, and being away from his family for the first time, he was lost, confused, homesick, and unhappy. He was assigned to one of the engine rooms of the *Missouri,* a 45,000-ton battleship. He was overwhelmed by the complexity of the engine room the first time that he stepped inside. He thought that he could never understand all the valves, pipes, and gauges. Then he discovered that he could get away without learning how to run the engine room. But he was so miserable and impatient to get out that he began to learn how to run the engine room just to pass the time and endure his predicament. It was a discouraging experience. He often felt that he would never learn, but he kept at it. An amazing thing happened: life in the navy became meaningful as he mastered the engine room. When he was able to run it, he had a sense of pride and accomplishment. He was needed. He could be depended upon. He still looked forward to the day when he would be discharged and go home, but it was not a looking forward in despair. A person may be tempted to run away from responsibility, yet it is the shouldering of that responsibility that leads toward meaning.

My kind of church will encourage a person to be

a responsible participant, first of all, by trying to find a job for him. Each person will be asked to help, if only in a small way, to make the church run. I believe that the average person only benefits from his activities in the church if he has some responsibility for keeping it going. It then becomes "my" church rather than "their" church. Also I believe that we encourage people to become responsible participants in the social order by being responsible in the church, the attitudes developed spilling over into their whole life.

People are not all the same. Therefore it is important to get them in the jobs that suit them best. A few years ago there was a lot of talk about how lay people are misused because they are asked to be ushers. I was in a church once when one of the men had been head usher for years—and he found great satisfaction in seeing that the ushering was well done. Here was a job that gave a man an opportunity to make a useful contribution. Ushering is a good job in the church, but if a person wants to do more than help with the ushering, it is wrong if he does not have that chance.

The goal of the church will be to get people to see that every job is needed and of value. In the congregation in which my wife grew up, there was an argument one time over who would start the fire on Sunday morning. Most of the members felt that it was beneath them. Finally, the most prosperous and successful farmer in the congregation said, "I'll start the fire. There are a lot of things that I can't do. I can't teach Sunday school and I sure can't preach, but

I can make sure that the place is warm." In a society that puts such heavy emphasis on status, my kind of church will seek to bear witness to the dignity of a needed job well done, that the competent garbage collector has a higher status than the incompetent executive.

Our society usually measures a person's contribution on the basis of the amount of money he earns. The person who does not have a paying job is often seen as a noncontributor. In my kind of church the emphasis will be on the basis of the service rendered, not the money made.

The example to be followed will be that of Jesus at the last supper. There was no servant there to wash the feet of the supper guests, as was often the custom, so Jesus got up and did it himself.

In order to be a responsible participant in society, a person needs to be generous, willing to share his time and money. But generosity is the most difficult attitude to develop. In a church made up of half-hearted Christians, this will be a major problem. Most of us will have ten thousand reasons why we can't be generous. I am not sure that we can even dent that problem. We will have to spend a lot of time reminding each other of Jesus and the generosity that we should have.

If people are to have responsibility in the social order, they need to do something about the problems of society; this means being involved in things outside of the church. No matter how good a society may be, there are always things wrong with it, and people in it who have unmanageable problems. Encouraging others to volunteer to work on these problems will be a major emphasis in my kind of church, but we will be realistic about it. The ecclesiastical quality-control experts have made this a major reason for their condemnation of church members, so small a percent can be enlisted for these kinds of activities. They have overlooked the fact that many members have problems as big as those of the people that the church should be helping, and many members because of age, health, or work are limited in what they can do, and that many without some direction don't know how to help. Some of the ecclesiastical quality-control experts are not sure what to do either. So my church will work on recruiting people for involvement in social concerns as a problem to be solved, not a condition to be condemned.

Obviously the biggest opportunity that most church members have to shoulder responsibility in the social order is in their work—and I would be quite inclusive here, including students and housewives as well as employed people. It also should be obvious that the kind of role one can play depends on his position in the social order—a person who is a president of a large corporation is in quite a different position than a person who is one of the janitors. Many people lament as inexcusable the failure of others to apply their Christianity to their work, but it seems to be exceedingly difficult. I have noticed that many of us ministers do a lousy job of being Christian in our work. My kind of church will have to put a lot of effort into discovering ways in which to help people apply Christianity to their work.

Many years ago in a small village most of the men hunted deer in the fall. A group of them kept pestering a nonhunter until he agreed to go. On the first day, he was stationed at a likely spot. As he waited, a big buck came down by him. When the drivers came through, the man hollered, "You should have been here. A big buck came by just before you got here." One of the drivers said, "What's that in your hands?" The man looked down at the gun, and only then did he realize that he should have shot the deer.

The temptation is always to look for someone else to do the job and forget one's own responsibility. My kind of church will be organized to continually remind the members that Jesus has called us to service in the world.

The church I have in mind will have a witness for the world. It will not draw the sharp division some people like to draw between a ministry to members and a mission to the world. The members are of the world and we will seek to draw in as many people as possible from the world. When my church helps people cope with life, develop a broader point of view, and become responsible participants in the social order, it is engaged in a mission to the world. But here I want to talk about the witness to that part of the world that is not a part of this church.

Such a witness to the world will begin with the assumption that it has never been perfect and won't be in the foreseeable future. If God wants a perfect world now, then he's going to have to do something different about it from what he has been

128

doing so far. Frantic hand-wringing about the state of the world is a waste of time. All that this church will try to do is bear a witness to the world, change what it can, and live in hope that God will use its witness and effort to bring in a better world.

Such a witness to the world will reject the good-guy–bad-guy approach that the people in the world can be easily divided into the righteous and the un-righteous. It will see that on both sides of most issues there are all kinds of people, from the best to the worst. It will recognize that many problems in the world are not just the result of evil intentions. The good intentions of incompetents can just as surely pave the road to hell as the worst intentions of malicious people.

Such a witness to the world will also reject the stance of moral arrogance. This church will state what it believes to be true, recognizing that it could be wrong. It will have no hot line to God. Neither will it condemn those who disagree. During World War I a prominent minister made the statement from the pulpit, "If a person is not heart, mind, and soul in the Allied cause, there is no room for him in the kingdom of man or in the kingdom of God." That was the war when the more Germans a person killed, the more Christian he was.

This witness to the world will be a witness against violence, because violence has no power to redeem, reform, or renew. Violence, no matter how well intended, is the pathway to death, not to life. Violence begets violence. It only creates new hatred and bitter-

129

ness, only pushes farther into the future the solution to the problem of people learning to live together in peace. Violence and its threat generate fears that open the door to war. Those who see violent revolution as the hope of the world see only a mirage that will vanish into the burning sands of the desert. Those who pursue violence are condemning the world to more years of hell, and perhaps to the final conflagration. Violence may stamp out one injustice, but a hundred will spring up to replace it. Violence as salvation is the illusion of well-intentioned fools who know no history. I understand how tempting violence is to the person crushed by injustice and how cruel he feels it is to oppose the only way he sees to end the injustice. But long ago in the desert Jesus rejected the temptation to bring in the kingdom of God through violence, through conquering the world with armed might, because he saw that God's kingdom will never come that way.

One must be realistic about violence in a world where many people, because of sickness of mind or maliciousness of heart, do evil. I think it naïve to believe that such people can be deterred by passive and patient kindness. We find ourselves forced on occasion to use violence and the threat of violence, because either of these may be the lesser of two evils. But at their best they only restrain evil and hold the gate shut against chaos. Violence is no answer, whether it is the nightsticks of the police, armies fighting to make the world safe for democracy, or revolutions to overthrow tyranny. A world that can find no other answer to injustice than violence must surely die.

A few years ago I was deeply concerned about a budget-cutting effort in the state legislature. I called a member of the legislature and explained to him very reasonably and calmly why I thought such a budget cut to be unwise. When I was finished, he said, "Art, you must remember, you're just a whisper in a hurricane." After I hung up the phone I pondered his comment. "All right," I said to myself, "I will be the whisper in the hurricane."

My kind of church will bear witness to the belief that the whisper is more powerful than the hurricane, that reason can conquer emotional irrationality. It is reason guided by fairness that has made the world better, not blind emotionalism, no matter how good its goal. People become human when they are moved by reason, not senseless passion. Reason seeks understanding, truth, and appreciation for others. Emotional irrationality seeks only the gratification of its wants, not caring for and not heeding those stomped under foot in the rush. Reason, if it is true reason, is compassion expressed, justice implemented, help rendered, and the rights of others recognized. Reason is the sharing of diverse insights, the reconciling of conflicting differences, and the providing of a place for every group in a world of fairness.

This witness will seek dialogue with all people. This church will recognize that decisions in this world are usually choices between alternatives, not absolutes. Realizing that one imperfect alternative may be as

Christian, or no more evil than another, it will understand that followers of Jesus can in good conscience be on opposite sides of an issue. In a world splintered, with each group clinging to its position as the only right one, it will work for negotiation and compromise. It will seek the greater truth that comes when the pieces of truth are put together. It will call the world to the exploring of new ideas and to a commitment to the search for truth rather than to half-truths, prejudices, and pride. It will seek open and respectful debate between divergent points of view.

My kind of church will live by the belief that a good compromise that enables conflicting groups to dwell together in reasonable harmony is better than principle rigidly pursued.

Perhaps the belief in the power of the whisper is the naïveté of fools. The hurricane of emotional irrationality may always prevail over the whisper of reason. The whisper may have no future. While I believe it does, I cannot be absolutely certain. If the whisper has no future, then the world has none either. If disaster is our lot, then I would rather keep the rendezvous with disaster as the whisper than as part of the hurricane. And I seek a church that will so live, and die if need be.

I will make no grandiose claims for my kind of church as the true church. I am not certain. When the final assessment is made, God may mark us down as having failed completely. All I can say is that my kind of church will seek to be a fellowship for failures; a refuge for the misfits in the army of the Lord;

a place where we can know Jesus as friend, enemy, and leader and hopefully, if only in small measure, do his will in the world. Many may say, "How far you are from Jesus!" And I will answer, "Yes, but we are nearer than when we started."

9.

The Church as Is, Can Be, and Won't Be

I ain't actually going to start a church for sinners, seekers, and sundry non-saints. I'll tell you why. I would be the first member and you would probably want to be the second. It would be wrecked right there. Between the two of us we would bring in all the faults that the church has now. We'd be right back where we started. My kind of church is a practical ideal.

Before I explain to you what I mean by a practical ideal, I want to say something about what I believe to be the biggest mistake that a lot of people make in thinking about the church; the mistake of confusing the purpose and the nature of the church, of identifying as nature what is really purpose. Purpose describes what the church should be; nature describes what the church is in the world. When one uses theological language, one is describing the purpose of the church. If one wants to describe the nature of the church, he must use nontheological terms. When one says, "The church is the body of Christ," he is talking about the purpose of the church. Its purpose is to be the body of Christ; its nature is an organization of people in the world.

Consider for a moment, "The church is the people of God, the community of the redeemed, brought into being by the life, death, and resurrection of Jesus, and inspired by the Holy Spirit to respond to Jesus and serve Him in the world." Now one could search until hell freezes over and he still would not find anything in this world that would fit that description, because it is a description of the purpose of the church and not its nature. If anyone, be he the most dedicated church member or the most indifferent-to-the-church person, were to look for the church in any place, he would start looking for a building that looks like most churches do. A description of the nature of the church has to make it possible to find an example of the church.

If we use the word *church* to refer to congregations as examples of the church in the world, one description of its nature would be: a church is an organization of people that usually owns a building with certain traditional characteristics, that meets at least once a week for worship, and engages in other activities usually involving the use of the building. With that description a person could find a church.

Let me give some other descriptions of the nature of the church.

135

A few years ago I was talking with an Episcopal layman. He was telling how the parish to which he belonged doubled its giving in one year. An advertising executive volunteered to be chairman of the annual fund-raising drive. After studying the situation, he told the pastor, "We're going to double our giving next year."

The pastor, surprised by the statement, asked, "How will you do that? We've tried everything and people just won't give any more."

The chairman replied, "Most of the people in this parish are very well-to-do. They belong for the same reason they belong to the country club—prestige— and they're going to pay accordingly." And they did.

What is the nature of that parish? It is the religious equivalent of the country club.

A few months ago I heard a group of ministers talking about a well-known, large congregation that recently had called a new pastor. Someone pointed out that the membership had decreased since the new pastor came. Someone else said, "Why, that's only natural. A lot of people join because they like a pastor. Some of them won't like the personality of the new pastor. There is always a decrease in membership until the new pastor can recruit people who like him."

What is the nature of that congregation? It is an organization of people in which there is a good personality fit between the pastor and people.

In many small rural communities, the church is the last surviving institution. The school, stores, and post office are gone. For members of such a congregation the church is the last symbol and evidence that this is a place, a community.

What is the nature of such a congregation? It is the last hold-out against the flood of change.

I point all this out not to criticize the church or to deny that God has a purpose for it, but to try to bring us to see things as they really are. It is inevitable that nature and purpose be different, that there be a gap between them.

It is impossible for people, or for most people, to see particular churches as other than organizations of people. When I went to work for the State Council of Churches and we moved to Syracuse, for the first time in our lives my wife and I had to decide what church we would attend. We had to go shopping for a church. Each church claimed to be in ministry for Jesus. We could not make a decision on the basis of Jesus having called us to be members of his church. We had to make it on the basis of distance, the kind of building, the personality and outlook of the pastor, the kind of program, and our reaction to the members.

No matter what theologians may say, people draw a distinction between belonging to *the* church and to *a* church. At the most, a commitment to Jesus says that a person should belong to a church, but it never says which one. A good illustration of this is what many a person does when he gets mad. He goes to another church. He is looking for a church that reflects the church as he understands it. While being a Christian requires a person to go to a church, it does not dictate which one.

137

I have concluded that many ministers become frustrated and disillusioned because they have never sorted out the difference between purpose and nature. Seeing purpose as nature, they become resentful when they discover that people have joined a church because it's a symbol of prestige, or because of the popularity of the pastor, or its the last survivor in the flood of change, or a variety of other reasons. Nature always describes the given with which a pastor must work; purpose provides the goals for his ministry. His task is always that of discovering ways by which the purpose can be realized, if only fleetingly, in the midst of its nature.

For instance, a few years ago my brother Fran was pastor of a congregation that had not paid its benevolence commitment because it did not have enough money that year. Many people seemed to feel that their responsibility to support the church meant that they had to see that the local bills were paid. If the church had a profit, then that could be used toward benevolences. Toward fall the church received a sizeable bequest, and it was up to the trustees to decide how to use it. A great discussion took place among the trustees as to how the money should be used. My brother pointed out to the trustees that the benevolences had not been paid. The purpose of a church was to have a mission of outreach, and this was one way it could have such a mission. He was able to persuade the trustees to use what was necessary to pay the benevolences, that this was just as much a bill as paying for the fuel. A number of people in the congregation questioned such a use of a bequest, but the decision was defended on the basis of the purpose of the church. My brother was effective at that point because he had clearly in mind the difference between purpose and nature, and because he was able to use a decision-making situation to illustrate and implement the purpose. If he had just sat around and growled because the congregation was not a reflection of the purpose, he could not have accomplished what he did.

Nature is where we are; purpose is where we hope to go.

In describing my kind of church, I dealt only fleetingly with purpose. I dealt primarily with process and organization, the church as a place where people could be helped to know Jesus-as-friend, to live with Jesus-as-enemy, and to follow him as leader. Even if my kind of church could be realized, it would still not fully reflect the purpose of the church. For instance, it would still not be made up of people fully obedient to Jesus. It would be an organization in which the conditions were best for the development of Christians, an organization in which I believe we could accomplish significant things to illustrate and implement the purpose of the church. But it would still be a church in the process of becoming what God intended it to be.

I have called my kind of church a practical ideal. Now I want to explain what I mean by a practical ideal. A practical ideal is a mental picture, a conceptualization, a model, a dream, a vision of what a person or a group would like to see as truth or reality. This is how I wish the world or a piece of the world really was. A practical ideal has five characteristics.

First, it helps a person to deal with life as it is and does not cause him to flee from life.

Second, it has specific suggestions on how the present situation can be improved.

Third, it cannot be fully realized in this world.

Fourth, it makes it possible to measure accomplishment and distance.

Fifth, it feeds meaning back into the imperfect present.

Several years ago when my brother Paul lived in Horseheads, New York, and I in Indiana, my family visited his one summer. Paul took me to the basement—bare walls, furnace, laundry tubs, and boxes. In the midst of the mess was a pile of lumber. Paul, who is a genius with his hands, had decided to build a game room. He carefully explained to me his plans. In spite of all he said, all I could see was a mess made worse by a senseless pile of lumber; but I realized that as he talked he no longer saw the basement as it was, but as it would be. He had a practical ideal.

He could have dreamed of building a mansion, but it would have done him no good. He could do something to make the house in Horseheads better, but he couldn't have built a mansion. His ideal was practical because it began where he was and it dealt with the world as is. He had specific plans in mind as to how he would reach the ideal. As he worked he could measure how much he had accomplished and how far he had to go. During the winter as he worked, he was constantly encouraged because he could see in his mind the game room completed. But he did not fully realize his practical ideal. The next summer, when we were there, he showed me the game room. To me it was beautiful, exactly what he had in mind. But no, he had made a little mistake here and one there—mistakes that I finally detected after he pointed them out to me. He had had to make a few minor adjustments, so it wasn't exactly as he had envisioned it.

I believe that we can only make things better as we develop practical ideals and seek to implement them.

A practical ideal must always make it possible for a person to deal with life as it is and not cause him to flee. We are in a period of nostalgia, a looking back on the past with fond memories. I find nostalgia very appealing. I grew up in Cherry Valley, a small village in upstate New York. I find great enjoyment in reminiscing about my growing up there. Sometimes, when the present is too much for me, I wish that I were back there. Some people like to argue that the past was not as good as my memory of it, which is true. (Whether the past was any worse than the present is another question.) But the fatal flaw in yearning for a return to the past is not my distortion of it; it is the fact that it is past. History cannot be repealed. Even if I could prove that the past was better than the present, the attempt to return to it would still be a fleeing from life rather than a dealing with it. A practical ideal must always enable me to deal with the world as is and to move into the future.

141

It must always start where I am and go in the direction that I'm going, no matter how far it takes me.

My church for sinners, seekers, and sundry non-saints is a practical ideal; I deal with the world as it is. I am not yearning for a return to some golden period in the history of the church or for the church to be in any kind of situation other than the one we have now.

A practical ideal must have specific suggestions on how the present situation can be improved. It must always have in mind a series of steps to be taken, decisions to be made, and activities to be done. I don't know how to make the church the body of Christ. I don't know how to make people fully Christian. I do have some ideas on how to bring together a mother whose son was killed in Vietnam and a mother whose son fled to Canada. I do have some ideas on how to engage the world in dialogue. I have specific things in mind that I can do and that I believe have a high degree of probability of making a contribution for Jesus.

A practical ideal cannot be fully realized in this world. I have no illusions about realizing my kind of church in this world. With my kind of people we would be in a real mess a lot of the time. Good feelings would collapse into fights, dialogue would be consumed by diatribe, and kindness would fall prey to selfishness.

A practical ideal makes it possible to measure accomplishment and distance. My kind of church will always be looking for new members. If we had more at the end of the year than at the beginning, we would have accomplished something. If we had twenty fights last year and nineteen this year, we would know that we were moving in the right direction, but still had a long way to go. We could tell whether we had engaged the world in dialogue, or failed.

A practical ideal feeds meaning into the imperfect present. My brother saw not the mess, but the game room. He could stand the confusion because he saw the game room coming into being. So also I see the church not as it is but as it can be. I can endure the mess, because I believe that the church can be different from what it is. I see the scattered pieces of a church for sinners, seekers, and sundry non-saints, and in my mind the scattered pieces are all put together in their proper places and are full of life.

At the beginning of the book I said that the church was not my home, and it cannot be my home. Home is my permanent place of living. Like Abraham of old, I am on a pilgrimage. The true pilgrimage I am on is not the one to disappointment, which I told you about. That was just a temporary diversion, a side trip. My true pilgrimage is one with Jesus through this life. We get separated because I am a straggler, but we meet each other again, because he is a friend seeking me out. I look forward to the community that has foundation, whose builder and maker is God. My home is there. No, the church cannot be my home, but it could be my tent—a place of shelter, renewal, and inspiration as I pause on my pilgrimage —a place where I could be helped to know Jesus-as-friend, live with him as enemy, and follow him as

143

leader. I look not for a perfect church. I look for a fellowship of failures, a church for sinners, seekers, and sundry non-saints who share with each other the good news of Jesus, who say over and over, "If we didn't have Jesus, we'd have to invent him."